The Vacant Seat

By Branislav Jaksic

TEACH Services, Inc.
PUBLISHING
www.TEACHServices.com

World rights reserved. This book or any portion thereof may not be copied or reproduced in any form or manner whatever, except as provided by law, without the written permission of the publisher, except by a reviewer who may quote brief passages in a review.

This book was written to provide truthful information in regard to the subject matter covered. The author assumes full responsibility for the accuracy of all facts and quotations as cited in this book. The opinions expressed in this book are the author's personal views and interpretation of the Bible, Spirit of Prophecy, and/or contemporary authors and do not necessarily reflect those of TEACH Services, Inc.

This book is sold with the understanding that the publisher is not engaged in giving spiritual, legal, medical, or other professional advice. If authoritative advice is needed, the reader should seek the counsel of a competent professional.

Copyright © 2012 Branislav Jaksic and TEACH Services, Inc.
ISBN-13: 978-1-57258-923-0 (Paperback)
ISBN-13: 978-1-57258-924-7 (ePub)
ISBN-13: 978-1-57258-925-4 (Kindle/Mobi)

Library of Congress Control Number: 2012948605

Published by
TEACH Services, Inc.
P U B L I S H I N G
www.TEACHServices.com

TABLE OF CONTENTS

Acknowledgements and Appreciation		v
Prologue		7
Chapter 1	Marriage: Keeping Tradition	9
Chapter 2	A Gathering of Clouds	13
Chapter 3	Unwanted Pregnancy	16
Chapter 4	Zivan Returns	22
Chapter 5	Years of War and Years of Peace	25
Chapter 6	Return to Hell	28
Chapter 7	Eating Organic	33
Chapter 8	The Church	35
Chapter 9	Another Sabbath Test	39
Chapter 10	First Move to Leave	41
Chapter 11	The Second Attempt	46
Chapter 12	The Third Attempt	50
Chapter 13	Taking Two Weeks Vacation	53
Chapter 14	The Escape	60
Chapter 15	Goodbye, My Friend	65
Chapter 16	Settling into the New Camp	71
Chapter 17	Registration to Immigrate	73
Chapter 18	Arriving in Australia	76
Chapter 19	My First Job in Australia	79
Chapter 20	Meeting Old Friends	81
Chapter 21	Buying My First House	83
Chapter 22	Getting Serious About Marriage	85
Chapter 23	Promotions at Work	90
Chapter 24	The Call to Work for the Lord	92
Chapter 25	A New Start	94
Chapter 26	Children's Upbringing and Education	96
Chapter 27	Meeting Her Majesty Queen Elizabeth	100
Chapter 28	Going "Home"	102
Chapter 29	The New Church	106
Chapter 30	Working in the Pacific Region	108
Chapter 31	Experiences	112
Chapter 32	Work in Other Pacific Region Countries	118
Epilogue		126

Acknowledgements and Appreciation

It is with deep felt appreciation that I acknowledge the tender love and guidance of my late mother who instilled in me her faith and a love of God, the creator of all. For me she was, and still is, a pillar of faith and strength. I will value that to the end of my life.

I also wish to thank my dear wife Mary who has stood by me for almost fifty years despite our different cultures and upbringing.

To my dear children—Alexander, Wilfrid, and Esther—of whom I am (we are) very proud of indeed. All three are medical practitioners, and they have made their lives useful, serving the communities in which they live. They help others who suffer in pain. It is my children who inspired me to write this story. As the years have passed, I have spent many hours telling them "my stories," and they have urged me to put it all in writing. Now my story is in writing and will not be forgotten.

And last, but not least, I wish to give hearty thanks to Tara Downey, director of Angel Blue Marketing. Tara helped re-write my book into the English language after I had written it in "my English," and she also encouraged me to publish it as my original intention was to just write something for family and friends. So, Tara, thank you indeed.

Branislav "Brian" Jaksic.

Prologue

The horses galloped along the dusty Serbian village road pulling the wagon that held the gravely ill Mila. They hoped to reach the nearby village where "Doctor Ana" practiced her healing art of curing all types of disease.

Mila, a mother of three, was dealing with an unwanted pregnancy. So she tried to terminate the pregnancy herself with instructions from an old "experienced" woman in the village.

Mila was not successful, so she had turned to Doctor Ana, the "one-legged woman," a name she acquired after losing a leg from gangrene. The condition, however, did not stop her from practicing her "art of healing." As soon as she had recovered from the amputation, she continued to perform all kinds of self-proclaimed cures. But she specialized in terminating unwanted pregnancies.

It was clearly controversial work. Many villagers viewed her with suspicion and avoided her, labeling her "evil and accursed." But Doctor Ana had a tough skin and ignored those remarks, continuing her practice, which brought in generous financial returns. Tragically for young Mila the treatment was complicated by infection, which was followed by blood poisoning.

She quickly became gravely ill and lay unconscious in the back of the wagon as the horses galloped back, finally coming to a stop in front of her comfortable home in the village.

The gates opened and as the wagon entered the courtyard, Mlia's children let out a shrieking wail. "Is she dead? Is our beautiful mother dead!? Wake up, dear mother! Wake up! Do not die, oh do not die!!"

Their urgent calls seemed to penetrate the unconscious mind of Mila, who had been lying in a fetal position.

She awoke, stretched herself out, and in a grave but firm voice exclaimed, "Why did you wake me up? It is not easy to drink the cup of death twice!"

And with this she exhaled her last breath. Mila, a beautiful mother of three children, at the age of thirty-six years, was dead.

"Mother, do not go," the children cried. "Please do not leave us. Oh dear Mother! Mother! Mother! Do not go, come back!"

But she was gone.

The funeral procession was around two kilometers long as hundreds came to pay their last respects to Mila who had been born into a very wealthy Jewish family in a nearby village and had married a middle class farmer and businessman, Lazarus Stefanovic.

The Vacant Seat

Lazarus owned a semi-precious stone mine with some of his Jewish friends and was well-respected in Krchedin, a village of 5,000 people. He even became the mayor of town for nine years. He was a very successful farmer, and as mayor he made much progress and brought prosperity to the village and its population.

Krchedin sits at the foot of the beautiful hill Frushka Gora. Just beyond the hill flows the mighty river Danube, the longest river in Europe. Many famous authors and musicians have written books and composed songs and musicals about the magic of the Danube.

The village lies three kilometers beyond Frushka Gora in a fertile plain where corn grows up to three meters high. Lovely pastures and good vegetable gardens, as well as sweet grapes and other fruit, grow in abundance, making Krchedin a very pleasant place to live.

After Mila died, the oldest child, Rada, fifteen years old, and her two brothers, Elias, thirteen, and Svetar, eleven, would go daily to the "little garden" behind the shed and pray, pouring their sorrows to Mila, who they believed was watching them from heaven.

After two years, their father, Lazarus, married again.

The woman he married was the most wonderful Christian lady, a kind and loving stepmother, and while she could not replace their beloved Mila, she was certainly the best "mother" anyone could hope for. She cared for them, comforted them, and as a devout Christian, taught them to love Jesus.

Chapter 1

Marriage: Keeping Tradition

By now life for the kind and loving eldest child, Radoslava, or Rada as she was known, was going well. She was well educated in the art of weaving, sewing, and cooking. She spent her days socializing with the wealthy residents of the village.

She herself had inherited a fortune from her mother, 300,000 dinars, which in today's value would be well over $30 million.

She was nineteen years of age at the time and as was customary, it was time for her to be married. There were a number of wealthy suitors, not only from the farming community but also professional men who manifested their intention for her hand in marriage.

For Rada, the decision was not hers to make. As was the tradition, it was up to her father to choose her future husband, and then the marriage was arranged by the parents of the bride and groom. The parents took the task very seriously, and it was important to look at all aspects of suitability, including education, wealth, and status in the community. The couple themselves would not be informed of their impending nuptials until four or five days prior to the engagement being announced.

On the day Rada was told who her husband would be, she was happy and felt secure with her position at home as the loving daughter of a father who showered her with love and presents as he returned from his business trips.

She also enjoyed the love and affection of her stepmother who taught her about the love of God and of the resurrection for those who love Jesus. Those promises gave her hope of seeing her wonderful mother Mila again.

It was a Sunday afternoon when Lazarus knocked on her door and asked to talk. Rada was conversing with her friend Boja about some handcraft she had just completed when her father entered the room and asked if Boja would excuse them. As Rada saw Boja off, both were curious as to what was so important.

The Vacant Seat

As Lazarus and Rada sat alone in the room, without much introduction he announced, "On Sunday you are to be engaged and in a month's time there will be wedding."

When Rada heard her father's words, she felt as though she would faint. The shock was like an electric bolt from the clear sky.

Not knowing what to think she asked a simple question, important to her, "To whom am I getting engaged? Who is the man?"

"Zivan Jaksic," her father calmly responded.

Recognizing the name, Rada knew Zivan was a man of smaller statue whose mother had died when he was only five years old. Zivan's father George re-married a rather corpulent lady who didn't care much for young Zivan, nor for his four sisters.

And to make things worse in Rada's mind, Zivan was only seventeen years old and very much underdeveloped. He looked more like a thirteen-year-old boy, while Rada was tall and in all appearances a very beautiful young lady.

"No, father, no I cannot marry Zivan," she cried. "Please, father, do not do this to me."

However, there were no negotiations. The decision had been made, and as such, must be carried out. As tradition would serve, Rada had no choice but to marry Zivan Jaksic.

Zivan's father, George, was a very wealthy and much respected man in the community. His wealth exceeded that of Lazarus, and he too had served as mayor of the town for nine years. But more than that, George was also the biggest landowner in the district.

At all times he had more than thirty in-house servants and a great amount of livestock, including cattle, horses, and sheep, as well as all the latest in farm machinery. His household was likened to that of Job in the Bible. He commanded respect in the community. In fact, when he walked on the street, women and children bowed to him and men took their hats off and saluted him.

Sadly, his wife died early, and the woman he remarried was also a widow with a daughter from a previous marriage. All went well for a number of years until tragedy struck again. At just forty-five years of age, George became very ill, and within a few weeks he was dead, leaving behind five children, a wife, and a stepdaughter.

For young Zivan this was a devastating blow. At the time he was only fourteen years of age, and he was not as fortunate as Rada to have a kind and loving stepmother. While she wasn't cruel like many stepmothers were renowned to be, Zvan's stepmother, Mara, was negligent of her stepchildren, Zivan in particular. Most of her attention was concentrated on her own daughter, Ella.

This left young Zivan to do what he wanted and to enjoy his life as a wealthy young man, taking little responsibility. He took no interest in the large property, his servants, or his livestock. His lived a carefree life.

As his sisters came of age, they married and left home, leaving young Zivan with his stepmother and stepsister. He lived a life of ease, a life of neglect, and he had many friends to shower gifts on.

Marriage: Keeping Tradition

This was the man Rada's father had chosen for her. Her brothers were equally shocked. "NO! Big NO!" they told her. "Hit your fist on the table and tell our father NO, NO, NO!"

But the always obedient Rada couldn't do that, and with many tears and much sadness, she told her father she would fulfill his wishes and marry Zivan.

As wedding plans were carried out for the marriage of these two people from wealthy backgrounds, there were rumors of an affair between the parents, Lazarus and Mara; however, that was never proven. It was said to be a marriage to keep wealth "in the family," and Rada saw herself as the sacrificial lamb.

After a short engagement the wedding preparations went into full swing, and it was to be a wedding for future generations to talk about. In accordance with custom, the bride and groom personally invited the distinguished guests, including their closest relatives and leading townspeople. In the invitation each guest received a "wedding garment" consisting of a fine linen material, which was white in color. Like in Bible times, all the guests who received the garment were obliged to wear it to the wedding. To disregard it would have been an absolute insult to the bridal party.

After all the principle guests were invited, the invitation was then extended to all the townspeople, which meant everyone in the next town, about six kilometers away, and the next town, twelve kilometers away.

The invitations were sent via the town crier who went from street to street and town to town with a drum and a trumpet. When the people heard him they would come out to the street to hear what news he had to announce. As the townsfolk came outside, the crier, also known as "the drummer," would start to read his news in a loud voice. "Lazarus Stefanovic's daughter Rada and Mara Jaksic's stepson Zivan are to be married. ALL are invited to attend the celebration of their wedding. The feast will last for seven days. Come all, come everybody." He then traveled to the next town with the same message.

On the day of the wedding, the gates of the groom's house opened wide and the townsfolk started arriving. The tables were set up in the large courtyard with enough food to satisfy all. Hundreds of domestic animals and birds were slaughtered and thirty-year-old wine flowed as a river. As more and more people came, greater quantities of food and drink appeared.

Toward the end of the feast, the Orthodox Church priests arrived and the couple were officially married. After the marriage ceremony Rada and Zivan traveled to a secret destination on their honeymoon.

It was indeed a fairytale wedding that promised a bright and wonderful future.

After returning from their honeymoon, life appeared to be going well for the newlyweds. Zivan took the role of husband seriously, and Rada busied herself making acquaintance with the house staff. Two young maids were assigned to assist her in house work, and she was kind but firm with them, making sure the house was kept spotless and all the cooking and washing was handled.

The Vacant Seat

Two years into their marriage, Rada gave birth to a son, an heir. To honor the late George Jaksic, the child was named George. George was loved, and no indulgence or expenses were spared for this was the child that would be the heir to the combined wealth of his parents.

Four years later another son was born. Predrag, or Peter, was a name given by his Aunt Vera, the older sister of his father. Peter grew strong and preferred the outdoor life while George liked busying himself indoors with books. Both boys were the pride and joy of their parents and the whole household.

Another two years went by, and there was a great excitement in the Jaksic's household as a daughter was born. Aunt Vera stepped in again to suggest the name for the newborn girl.

"Branka shall be her name," announced Aunt Vera.

"Why Branka?" asked Rada.

"Well," Aunt Vera explained, "I know two very beautiful children, two most wonderful children, whose parents are most wonderful people. They are a striking resemblance to this lovely family, and their children's names were Predrag and Branka."

Rada readily agreed and George, Predrag, and Branka added much happiness to the whole household.

Following this, life in the Jaksic family was good. The children were growing well. They were healthy, happy, and above all, doted on by their loving parents, aunts, uncles, and friends. It seemed the fairytale life would last forever.

Chapter 2

A Gathering of Clouds

In a fairytale it is difficult to imagine there could be signs of deterioration. But a greater hand was at work, and change was about to begin, altering the direction and the destiny for all existing members of the family and for generations to come.

Zivan, who in his youth lacked responsibility, started to show those elements in his character, something that would mar and eventually bring sadness and tragedy to the whole family.

Zivan was very set in his ways and would not tolerate instructions from his property managers, and he openly disregarded their advice and acted in defiance to their counsel, no matter how wise they were. Should they dare to press their point, Zivan would summarily dismiss them regardless of their experience or length of loyal service. He would quickly hire another manager and repeat the same behavior in a short time. This caused much distress to the rest of workers who were tired and confused with their master's actions.

When Rada would point out to him that what he was doing was causing difficulties among the workers, he would roughly dismiss her caution, and he even accused her of being infatuated with some of the managers.

More problems arose when he started to mix with people who loved to drink and get drunk. Until now, Zivan had been a social drinker, but with his new "friends" this started to change. More and more he organized lavish parties that his drinking buddies attended. These parties were drunken and debasing times, and Rada became more and more alarmed. All of her attempts to change his downward slide were ignored. He would go out and come home late, heavily intoxicated, and as the situation got worse, many of their loyal workers left to seek employment elsewhere.

Rada's father, Lazarus, also became worried and distressed at the situation his daughter was now in. All his attempts to help his now alcoholic and apparently hopeless son-in-law were ignored. Zivan even accused his father-in-law of fraud and deception. Her mother's inheritance, which Rada should have by now received, was not coming as her father had invested it in different projects, which were not bringing good returns.

The Vacant Seat

To help his daughter out of "hell," as he described it, Lazarus pleaded with her to leave Zivan and live in the house he had purchased with her money. He had also invested her money in a trout farm that began to bring healthy returns, which he promptly invested in other enterprises.

This situation added to the tension between Rada and Zivan.

Lazarus continued pleading with his daughter to leave the now continuously drunken Zivan. He even confessed to her that he had made a terrible mistake with the arranged marriage and asked earnestly for forgiveness.

After considering her father's propositions, Rada decided to stay with her husband and carry the burden no matter what the cost would be. Zivan was becoming even more of an alcoholic, and as a result he became more and more abusive and violent. Rada now found herself in an unbearable situation. She tried to reason with him during the short times when he was sober, but all her pleadings were ignored.

She then turned to his uncle, Draga Jaksic, a wise man and a loving father who had high regard for Rada and often rebuked his nephew. In spite of warnings, pleadings, rebukes, and entreaties, Zivan continued his lifestyle—a lifestyle that could only lead to ruin and sorrow of his family.

Rada was becoming more and more stressed. She continued in vain to reason with him, but the more she pleaded the worse he got. With his drinking he started having affairs, and he did not hesitate in telling Rada that these women were much better than her. With the neglect of work and care of the fields, the shortages started to be felt. The harvests were smaller, and the crops did not yield as they had in the past. In order to maintain his lifestyle, Zivan started selling some of the land and houses he had inherited. This brought even greater stress on Rada who, by now, was regularly attending church with her stepmother. She felt comforted among the people at the church and found that her faith in Christ enabled her to bear the burden of having to live with an alcoholic husband.

In the winter of 1937 Rada developed a cough that would not go away despite all efforts on her part. She turned to doctors who became concerned with her condition and sent her to a clinic for more thorough examination.

To her horror, she was diagnosed with tuberculosis (TB) or consumption disease as it was called then. She knew that being diagnosed with such a disease meant almost certain death because at that time thousands suffered from this scourge, and there was no known cure. Some of her relatives and friends had suffered and died after a short time.

Rada's trust in God was now severely tested. She continued going to church, but her hopes of survival faded by the day. She spent most of her day in bed gasping for breath, and while her children felt the suffering of their mother, they were too young to do much to ease her sorrows.

Zivan showed no sympathy, nor did he help her in the house or with the children. She had to rely on the help of her stepmother who was already overburdened with other members of the family. Zivan's stepmother had moved away with her daughter, taking a good part of the family's wealth with her, and she rarely visited.

By now the land was almost split in half and some other properties that should have come her way, including the inheritance from her mother, never came. It also became known that her brothers had also played a part in defrauding her of what rightfully belonged to her.

By this time Zivan seemed to have lost all sense of reality and all the responsibility as husband and father.

Rada dreaded his coming home, for when he arrived he was always drunk, bringing with him unreasonable demands, violence, and accusations against her father and brothers. He even accused her of unfaithfulness as a wife. This situation added more suffering to her already emaciated body, and as the TB progressed, Rada prayed more earnestly for divine intervention. Sadly, there was no help, and she started counting down the days in anticipation of death.

In the midst of that horror, one particular night Zivan came home half-drunk and in an unbearable and violent state. As the night progressed, he demanded that Rada submit herself to him. Despite her pleadings, he forced himself very violently onto her, causing her frail body severe pain.

During and after this horrific ordeal, Rada was only semi-conscious, and it took her a long time to recover enough to get out of bed and prepare food for her hungry and crying children. Following the horrific assault, Zivan left early in the morning and did not return home for weeks. It was good for Rada as his absence gave her time to recover somewhat and to look after the children as much as she could with her health as bad as it was, but as the days passed her health continued to deteriorate to such an alarming state that with each bout of coughing blood would appear in her sputum. She consulted a doctor who was Zivan's first cousin, his aunt's son. Bora was a very well-known physician and was well-respected in the community. He felt for Rada and tried his best to help her professionally and personally. Bora and his wife often helped with the children or with cleaning and washing .

The doctor gave her little hope of survival.

Chapter 3

Unwanted Pregnancy

After the horrific assault by her husband on that darkest of the nights, Rada tried to put the terrible ordeal behind her, and if possible, by the grace of God to whom she now prayed earnestly, she sought to forget what happened.

She did not think twice about the possibility of pregnancy, not even a few weeks later when her monthly cycle did not occur. She assumed that because of her illness she had missed her period. But as time went on and her period did not return, she became concerned.

Thinking the worst, she consulted her doctor. Upon examination Bora confirmed her worst fears. Rada was pregnant. Stunned, fear gripped her, and her mind seemed to spin. She felt let down by God and by everyone. All human reasoning momentarily left her. Tears ran down her cheeks that she could not control.

She had no idea what to do next. Would she follow the same path her mother had gone down even though she had died in the process? Perplexity and confusion took hold of her now very fragile body, and she started shaking uncontrollably. Realizing her grave condition, Dr. Bora and his wife embraced her and held her in their arms until the shaking stopped.

After that they put her in bed where she rested for some time. They brought her food and encouraged her to eat in order to gain back her strength. After recovering enough to go home to her waiting children, she prayed earnestly for strength and wisdom on how to deal in this almost unbearable situation.

Returning home, Zivan was in a very sullen mood. He refused to talk to Rada and was rough and impatient with the children, but after a few days he seemed to become more tolerant, and Rada decided it was time to tell him that as a result of his attack on her she was pregnant.

Upon hearing the news, Zivan flew into a fit of rage so great that anyone within close proximity had to flee to avoid harm. He grabbed a chair and hurled it at Rada. But her quick reflexes saved her from being seriously hurt. He continued yelling obscenities at her and accusing her of being a whore, claiming the child was not his.

"Whore! Whore!" he yelled. "Serves you right! Now you are going to die. This is sure. This is the best news I've heard. You will burn in hell and that child of yours and your lover will burn together with you."

With more cursing and swearing he left as he always did when he was faced with any difficult situation.

Although Rada felt completely forsaken and rejected by all, there was still a flicker of hope. As a firm believer in God, she believed He would help her find a way out, even if it meant death. In fact, to Rada, death would bring a wonderful release.

Never had she entertained the thought of suicide, but at the same time she couldn't see a way out of her situation. So she sent a message to Dr. Bora and asked to speak with him as soon as possible. He arrived the following day and after a few preliminaries, he told her in very direct language that she had to terminate the pregnancy and "the sooner the better."

He gave Rada no options. If she wanted to live a little longer, terminating the pregnancy was her only option. In fact, there were no other options in his opinion.

"If you continue with the pregnancy, you will not last to give birth. You will die and the child will die. Why? Because of your condition," he said. "Let me be honest, dear Rada, you are dying. There is no cure for your disease, you are in the last stages of your sickness, and it would be indeed a supernatural miracle for you to survive long enough to give birth to that child."

This was the very thing Rada had been expecting from God. She knew she was dying. Her strength was ebbing away by the hour. She found it very difficult to move, to walk, to get dressed, to attend to the children, to cook, or to do anything at all.

She needed to rest in bed, but even there she would often gasp for breath, and when the coughing bouts attacked her emaciated body, she would fall back against the pillow, thinking that death was moments away.

But for some reason, death never came. She struggled with Dr. Bora's recommendation. She just felt that she could not go through with the termination. She gathered her last vestige of strength and went to the church to talk to the pastor.

The pastor was busy as it was a Sunday, and she had to endure hours of sitting in what to her was a very uncomfortable chair. The pastor spoke kindly to her when he approached, knowing her difficult situation with her sickness and marriage. He tried his best to put her at ease by offering a prayer for her before starting their conversation. He then asked her how she felt and offered her a more comfortable chair.

The Vacant Seat

At first Rada could not talk, tears ran down her cheeks uncontrollably. He put his arms around her, and his wife did the same. They both waited until she calmed down and was able to speak. She informed the pastor of her ordeal with her violent, drunken husband, and then she told them about the pregnancy. But she did not stop there. She continued, "Because of the state of my health, Dr. Bora insists I terminate the pregnancy immediately. That way I would have a slight chance to prolong my life a little longer."

The pastor listened attentively to Rada's story and to her terrible dilemma. After consultation with his wife and other trusted members of the congregation, the pastor came back to Rada who was by now feeling very anxious and physically weak. He sat next to her, and holding her hand, he told her very calmly that all lives are in God's hands and she should commit her life to God.

"If it is God's will that both you and the child will live, you will live, but if it is not His will, then either or both of you shall die," he said. "But should you both live, who knows what plan the God of heaven has for this child!"

These words did not alarm poor Rada. On the contrary, his words sounded prophetic. A strange calm came upon her, and she got up from the chair, thanked the pastor and his wife, and left the room. She started walking home, feeling as though she was in some kind of a trance. Her mind refused to think, as though she had taken a strong tranquilizer.

Although it was a two-kilometer walk she did not seem as tired as she normally was, and upon arriving home, she went into her day room and sat on a sofa. The decision came to her suddenly, and she said out loud, "I will keep the baby. I will go through with the pregnancy. I will tell this to Dr. Bora whether he approves or not." She then went to prepare food for the children who were anxiously waiting for their mother.

That same afternoon Dr. Bora came, not only as a routine visit but also to inform her that he was arranging for her to go to a clinic to terminate the pregnancy. Without asking her what her thoughts were on the matter, he went on to tell her everything had been arranged and he would bear the costs. To his astonishment, she replied simply, "I am going through with the pregnancy."

The doctor thought he was hearing voices. "What did you just say? You are going through with the pregnancy? How long do you think you will go?"

"Well it usually takes nine months," Rada calmly replied.

Upon hearing this, Dr. Bora asked her to bring him a hand washing basin and a towel. Rada, thinking that he needed to wash his hands, promptly brought the requested utensils and held the dish for him to wash his hands. As he put his hands in the water, he repeated Pontius Pilate's act.

"I, Dr. Bora, wash my hands of you since I do not wish to be responsible for the death of two people." Then he continued. "You will not see me again. Perhaps I shall see you at your funeral, but you will not know that I am looking at your dead body and that of your child."

He then left without saying goodbye. Rada was astonished at his words. But for a reason unknown to her, she made no attempt to talk to him, nor did she try to hold him back. Her destiny, according to the old pastor, now lay in God's hands. But despite that she still felt as though she had to do something. There was an elderly German doctor, Dr. Rener, in the village who was well reputed for his experience and his absolute care and dedication for his patients. Without any hesitation, Rada got up and walked to Dr. Rener's office, which was two doors down from her house. Although they knew each other as neighbors and often greeted each other, she had never been to him as a patient.

He knew of her illness, since neighbors do talk. He also knew Dr. Bora and had heard Rada coughing as she went past his house. He felt great sorrow for her, and at times, he felt that he should do something for her, but he restrained himself since she was being seen by another doctor who was well-known for his expertise in the art of healing.

As Rada entered the elderly doctor's examining room, she felt a kind of assurance and peace she had not felt for a long time.

"Is my case hopeless? Will my baby die in my womb?" she asked.

Looking at her emaciated body, her thin arms, her hunched back, and her stomach, Dr. Rener ignored her question and asked her his own questions.

"Do you want to live? Do you want your baby to live?" he asked. "If you want to live, we must do something about that cough. You are coughing too much and too loud. The neighbors may not like this; they are being disturbed."

Rada felt as if she was being mocked by the old man, and she started to leave.

"Where are you going?" he asked.

"I am going home to die," she responded.

"No, you are not going to die. What I meant to say is that we are going to fight against that enemy of yours, the one that is tearing apart your beautiful lungs and your whole body. And who knows? We may win."

This was a diagnosis Rada did not expect. Was this old doctor serious that there could be victory over this evil enemy in her body? Could she yet live to see her baby born? Would she be able to hold him in her arms, cuddle him, and kiss him? For the first time since she entered this dark tunnel of hopelessness, there seemed to be a flicker of a very small light.

"Dear Dr. Rener, do you think there is hope for me to fight against that enemy as you have described my sickness?" she asked.

"Yes, one should never give up hope of survival; one has to fight until the end, whenever the end may be." As the doctor spoke these words, Rada felt an aura of determination and even of final victory.

Rada was now in her fourth month of pregnancy, and the medication Dr. Rener prescribed, plus her new determination to live, seemed to be working. She felt her physical and psychological strength

The Vacant Seat

gradually returning, and she even allowed herself to indulge in better food, and she renewed friendships with some of her old best friends.

Dajka Jaksic was her closest friend, then Olga and a few others. For a time they seemed to stay away from her, despite it being a time when she needed them most, but they can be likened to the biblical story of Job and his friends—although they came and stayed with him, their stay was more of a burden to Job than help.

Rada was progressing nicely under Dr. Rener's care, and she was determined to live. Dr. Rener did the work not only of a physician, but he also kept telling her, "You will make it. God is on your side, and your children need a mother."

Her motherly instinct became a very powerful motivator in her determination to survive. She walked more every day, did some work in the garden, and above all prayed that God would extend her life at least long enough to see her children grow up. As she had a naturally happy outlook on life, there was usually a smile on her face—a smile that had almost disappeared during her darkest times. Now the smile was returning, and life was again something to fight for.

While purchasing medication on one occasion, after seeing her smiling face, the pharmacist told her something that greatly surprised her and at the same time gave her more zest for life. He told her, "Mrs. Jaksic, you will live."

With a smile she asked, "What makes you think that?"

"Well," he continued, "people who come here to buy this kind of medication obviously have the same sickness as you, but they are sullen and angry. They appear to blame the whole world for their plight, but you come here smiling. You will live."

Again she felt she was hearing prophetic words. And she did live.

The time arrived for her new baby to be born. Although six weeks early, the contractions started, and she sent an urgent call to the village midwife who arrived in a short time to deliver the baby—the baby who should never have been born; the baby who was rejected by its father; the baby Dr. Bora told her would kill her.

"It is a boy!" exclaimed the midwife. "You have another boy, Rada! A lucky lady, you now have three sons." She then added, "But this one will need special care. Being premature and with your sickness, he is very small and extremely thin, almost only skin and bones."

Before giving the baby to Rada, the midwife placed a mask over Rada's mouth as a precaution so she would not pass on her TB. In addition, because of her disease, she would never be able to breast feed her son. Rada was overwhelmed. She was alive; her precious new baby was alive.

"Oh God, you are a wonderful God! You have heard my cry. You have extended my life, and now dear God help me. Oh dear God, show more mercy to me and my dear new baby that we may both live," she prayed.

And with her prayer, she took the baby in her arms, and tears of joy mixed with sorrow flowed freely. The midwife gave her some instruction on how to handle her "very tiny baby" who weighed just under 1.5 kilograms, and Rada knew she would do all she could to preserve this precious life.

Since she was still very ill, her friend Dajka came to help her. She cooked, cleaned the house, and helped the oldest son, George, who was now eight years old, get ready for school.

Dajka did all she could for her sick friend. Sadly Rada's two brothers who were married with wives and could have given some assistance lived very much for themselves.

Lazarus was now gravely ill with throat cancer, and he didn't have much time to live. After some time, Elias, Rada's brother, came to visit her to see how she was. He was greatly surprised that she and the baby were indeed alive. He walked into the room where Rada and the baby were. But upon seeing the baby, he was aghast. Shocked, he couldn't restrain himself, "My dear sister, how could you give birth to such an ugly baby? This poor child, if he lives, will not be able to move among the people. He will not be able to walk the streets without wearing some kind of mask. The villagers will stare at him. How will he travel to the city or, if destiny would have it, the world?"

Rada did not address her brother's rather cruel comments, instead she said, "I will be happy if the Lord gives him health and life."

Without offering any help, Elias left.

Strangely, the last few words he spoke seemed indeed prophetic, for this "ugly baby" would someday "travel the world."

Chapter 4

Zivan Returns

Some months after his outburst when he denied the pregnancy was the result of his cruel attack on his very ill wife, Zivan returned. But before he was even settled back in the house, he went on the attack. When he saw the child, he was enraged, and he told Rada, "This kopile [bastard] could never be my child. He is not my child. Take him to his real father!"

Zivan then accused her of having an affair with a man in the village. Rada, however, had no words for such brutality, and she just held her baby firmly in her arms, protecting him in case Zivan was to lose control.

She was a woman of high morals, and an attack of this kind was cruel beyond any description. She simply told him God would be his and her judge and that He would vindicate her honesty and faithfulness. And God did.

To name a baby, it was custom to invite kumovi, marriage witnesses, to take the baby to the Serbian Orthodox Church where the baby would be christened and given a name.

According to the custom, it was the task of the kumovi to name the baby, but for this baby, Rada chose the name.

"His name will be Branislav. He will also be known as Branko."

The reason for the name was that Rada loved to read, and there was a very famous Serbian satirist Branislav Nusuc whose works she read, as well as a poet Branko Radicevic, whose poems she loved to read. She gave him the names in the hope that by giving those names, he would one day be a writer like these famous men.

I am Branislav-Branko, and I write this story with mixed feelings, feelings of sadness and feeling of joy. Rada, my mother, survived and was victorious in all the battles she was forced to fight.

She was a true hero; a true mother who was worthy of that noble name "Mother."

I shall return to her story later.

I am now seventy-four years old, and looking for that blessed hope of seeing my mother again at the second coming of our Lord and Savior, Jesus Christ. She died at 89 years of age.

After I was born, Rada and Zivan had two more children, daughters. Mira was born two years later, and the last one Milena, affectionately called Beba (meaning baby), was born six years later.

Zivan did not deny fatherhood of any of his five other children, only me. Zivan, unfortunately, was unable to give up his alcohol habit. It became part of his nature so much so that he was drunk more than he was sober. The attacks on our mother continued, both verbally and physically. She spent her life in a living hell, if such a location exists, and as we grew, we too felt the suffering with her.

To supply his constant need for alcohol, not being able to hold any job, Zivan started selling the inheritance of his famous late father, George. If George had known what his only son was doing, he would have found no rest in his grave.

Since his father left most of his estate to his son instead of his daughters, which was the custom, Zivan was able to sell all of it at his will, and no one could stop him.

This put our mother and us in a very volatile situation. We could have ended up homeless on the street, but luckily, things changed, and he stopped selling.

Around this time Zivan decided to part with us and move to Belgrade, the capital, to find "new happiness" with another woman and to buy a hotel. He laid this proposal before our mother, and having no options she had to agree. He demonstrated some generosity by proposing to divide all the properties he still had with her.

She, as he later admitted, was a good mother but not a good wife. After this proposal he moved quickly to fulfill his plans, and after selling his portion, he moved to Belgrade.

Mother finally got some peace from his tyranny, but sadly, the peace was not to last long. After six months he sent a message through some of his friends to "tell the whore to move out or I will kill her and her children. Her and her bastard child will die first."

When the threatening message reached Mother, she quickly moved across the road to a house that belonged to one of her distant relatives but was vacant. Not having time to move all her furniture and bedding, she took the most needed things.

The next day he arrived penniless. In six months, he had spent all of the money he had earned from selling his portion of the properties, which was a substantial amount. He now started selling our furniture and the bedding she had bought when she married him.

Neighbors, of course, were eager to buy the most beautiful and costly handmade articles for the bargain price he was offering. He would have sold everything had it not been for a young boy who came to our mother and told her, "Mr. Jaksic is selling all that is in the house, and the neighbors are buying it."

In her desperation to save some of her beautiful much-needed bedding and other household articles, she notified her brother Svetar who rushed to the house. Being physically strong, he literally threw out all the buyers. But more than that, he inquired as to who had already bought things, and he went to those houses, forced himself inside, and collected some of our mother's possessions. In the following

The Vacant Seat

years, however, as she visited some of the neighbors, she would often recognize some of the goods that had been bought from her drunken husband.

Soon after the sale, and as a result of the way it was stopped, in order to gain revenge, Zivan came to the house one evening and, in a fit of furious rage, broke all the windows in the house. It was a very cold winter, and since our mother could not afford to buy wood to heat the house, we were exposed to severe cold. The little wood she had, she used for cooking meals for us. After that, all six of us had no choice but to sleep in the kitchen.

Since Yugoslavia, as it was known at the time, was under German occupation, German police patrolled the streets every evening. As they passed our house one day, they inquired as to who had broken our windows.

At first our mother was reluctant to tell them for the fear of what they might do to Zivan, but the neighbors told the police who it was, and when they asked if it was true, she had to admit that it was our father who had done it. After apprehending him, they took him to the police station for questioning, and our mother went to the station to plead for him not to be harmed in any way. They promised they would not hurt him, but they said they would transport him to Germany to work in a factory since most of German men were engaged in the war.

Before he was taken to Germany, mother packed a case for him with food, clothing, and a Bible she hid under the clothes. She could not say goodbye to him as she was not allowed to visit him.

Without a goodbye, our father was gone.

Chapter 5

Years of War and Years of Peace

Our father stayed in Germany for nearly four years.

Soon after his departure, we returned to our home. It was in a devastating state and in need of urgent renovations. The pillars that held the house together appeared ready to fall. The roof leaked. The windows were broken, and there was no electricity as the power had been cut off because of unpaid bills. But our mother had no money for repairs.

It was the spring of 1942, and I was four years old. My oldest brother George was twelve, Predrag-Petar was eight, and my younger sister, Mira, was almost two years old. We came home with our mother who was overwhelmed by the burden of it all. She had a strong faith in God, but at the same time she was worried. Then, as if sent by God, her relative Dajka came and told her, "Your house needs repairs. You need warmth and food for those children."

Our mother knew all this, but she didn't know how to get any money. Then Dajka gave her a sum of money that would cover all the costs for the repair of the house and for food, clothing, and other needs. She was an angel from heaven. Our mother was forever thankful for Dajka's assistance.

During the time of our father's stay in Germany, our mother lived in peace. It sounds rather ironic for there was war raging all around yet she lived in her home, undisturbed by the one who should have been her protector and a caring father to her children.

Her health had greatly improved, she was stronger, had gained some weight, and under Dr. Rener's care had new hope of full recovery, something that remained a shock as thousands continued to die from the disease.

Despite everything she had gone through, our mother always put others ahead of herself. And in the darkest days of war, she endangered her own life and ours to hide some Jewish people in the attic. She told us that if we were ever asked if there were strangers in our house we should say, "No, there are no strangers."

It was not long after that instruction that German patrol officers were seen going from house to house searching for Jews or partisans, the resistance army. It was known that if they found anyone

The Vacant Seat

hiding these people, the whole family would be killed and the Jewish people would be taken to the gas chambers and exterminated. When the patrol came to our house, before asking any questions or searching the house, I called out, "We have no strangers in our house."

Fortunately for us, they did not hear me or were too intoxicated to hear, since in every house they were offered drinks, which was a positive thing because it meant that many of them were ineffective in their search.

It was 1945, and I was seven years of age. I remember the end of the German occupation of Yugoslavia. The Russian army was advancing from the east, and the German army was still holding the areas where we lived. The two forces met in and around our town. We had a kind of a bomb shelter where we used to run whenever the air raids came. This particular night was to be the last night of occupation, and all the German population had to leave and go to Germany.

We all ran into a secret bomb shelter, and most of our neighbors, relatives, and friends came. The reason I remember this particular night so well is because as children we were told all the Germans were leaving and by morning there would be no more Germans in our town. As we all settled in the shelter, a woman came in with a baby.

When the people in the shelter saw her, they knew everyone would be killed if the baby started crying and gave away their hiding spot. The woman pleaded to be allowed to come in, but there was no mercy shown. When our mother saw what was going on, she told the lady to hand her the baby. The lady handed her baby to our mother, and Mother told us that she would stay in the house for the night.

"The Lord will protect me," she told us as we pleaded with her to stay with us in the shelter. We feared that she would be killed, but she took the baby, and the bomb shelter door closed behind her.

I silently cried for the safety of my mother. During the night no one slept. We heard screams, gunfire, and bombs exploding. It was horrific, but by morning everything was silent.

As we emerged from our hiding place, we children were not allowed to go into the street. We were told that many people had died, and they had to remove all the bodies. The carnages of war were everywhere.

How many had died that night we were never told, but it must have been thousands, mostly soldiers, as the two armies met.

Our mother emerged from the house with the baby in her arms, both alive and well. Although I was only seven, I marveled at the faith and courage of our mother. She virtually sacrificed her life, not only for that baby but for all of us. By late afternoon we were allowed in the streets, and what we saw made us feel ill. Many houses had been damaged or destroyed, and nearly every house, including ours, had bomb and bullet holes throughout. There was no question in our minds that God had saved her and the baby.

During his stay in Germany, our father seemed to come to some kind of realization of the effects of his destructive ways on his family and himself. As a result he wrote many letters of repentance and asked our mother for forgiveness.

In his letters he promised that if she accepted him back, he would be a changed man, a different man, a good father to his children. He wrote about how God had protected him from certain death on numerous occasions.

He and some of his friends used to sleep under a large bridge, their shelter and accommodation. They felt quite safe there, but one night he dreamed that the bridge would be destroyed by a bomb. In the morning he warned his friends that they should move to another place since this bridge would be bombed. As he told them his dream, they laughed at him and called him a dreamer of doom.

The following night he found another shelter and was the only survivor of the group after a bomb destroyed the bridge they had called home. To him, that and a number of other incidences were a certain sign that God wanted to save his life so he could return to his family.

Mother was at first apprehensive as to his promises and his apparent change. Finally, she decided to give him another chance. After all, she thought, four years was long enough for a person to change his ways, particularly after all he had experienced in Germany—seeing carnage and suffering that human language could not fully describe.

All this gave her hope and some kind of assurance that changes had taken place in his life, and as a result, our mother reconciled with him. It was good for a while, but just before the birth of the youngest daughter, Melena-Beba, in 1946, signs of his old life started to appear. He started to revert back to his old ways. He began going out with some of his old drinking friends. He kept reassuring Mother she had nothing to worry about and that he was simply telling them about his experiences from Germany, but this was not the whole truth.

Our father keenly disliked our mother's brothers and cousins, for these men were now leaders in the post-war Communist government. He still regarded himself landowner and "capitalist"; he was strongly opposed to the Communist system of government. As soon as the Communists came to power, they made land reforms, taking the land from rich landowners and making zadruge communes. Declaring that all the land now belonged to the people, if anyone refused to voluntarily surrender their properties, it was confiscated.

This happened to our mother and father. They had virtually everything they owned taken from them and declared the "peoples." This resulted in our father's hatred against our mother's brothers and cousins.

One of my mother's cousins became president of the people's assembly of Vojvodina, which had no status as a state, but as a territory, which later become part of Serbia. Another cousin was chief justice, and the third was a high-ranking military officer. But despite all the hatred he had toward our mother's relatives, it was alcohol that enticed him to return to his old life.

Toward the end of our mother's pregnancy with Beba, she gave our father money to go to the city of Novi Sad to buy five liters of cooking oil. He was expected to return by 3:00 p.m. at the latest, but late that evening, he hadn't arrived. The next day we received news that he was not returning. The man who brought the dreadful news told our mother that the money she had given him for oil had been spent on drinks.

Chapter 6

Return to Hell

It is impossible to read someone's mind, but if it was possible, it would have been a great help to us to be able to know what our father was thinking.

He had rejoined our family after surviving the war years in Germany. God, according to him, had saved his life so he could be reunited with us. And yet he threw it all away and returned to a life of misery and drunkenness that caused his family sorrow and heartbreak.

By now we were growing, and George was sixteen years of age. Fortunately, our mother summoned all her resources and put him through higher education and university. Being a brilliant student, he achieved good grades and graduated with high distinction in civil engineering. Predrag went on to become a machine mechanic, and Branka went on to learn dressmaking.

I was eight years old when our father's fury against our mother returned. At the same time, he again started calling me kopile and denying me as his son. This had a profoundly negative impact on me, and I often felt resistance and even hatred toward him.

It was not so much his rejection of me but his total negligence of all of us. We were his children, and we needed him more then ever before. Our family's properties had fallen into communist hands; there was no money, not even for food, and yet my father was always able to find money to drink and live a life of complete negligence in regards to his family.

Had he left us in peace, life would have been much easier for our mother and for us. Instead, he often came home drunk, threatening to kill our mother and us.

We spent most of our time inside our house with the doors locked. At times, he would break windows, enter our home, and attack our mother for no reason. We would form a human shield around her to protect her, but unfortunately, we were not always successful.

I recall one time when Father came home half drunk with a large knife in his hand. With fury he went straight toward our mother. He was so quick that we had no time to form a shield around her. He hurled himself at her with the knife in his hand, intending to stab her right in the heart. But God did not allow our mother to die at his hands. As my father lifted his hand to stab her, Mother grabbed the knife by the sharp blade and managed to take it away from him. It was a life-and-death situation.

He tried to get the knife back from her. Her hand was bleeding heavily as a result of the cut she'd sustained when she grabbed it, but as he tried to wrestle it from her, we ran to her, and within minutes we were between them.

He stopped and told us to leave or he would kill us. But there was no way we would move. He then tried to hit and pull us away, but without success.

Realizing our determination, if need be to the death, he left the house cursing and threatening that he would finish us all next time he saw us. He told us he would cut us into pieces and throw us into the street.

My father was often short of money to supply his drinking habit, and in order to get some cash, he would "take" or steal things from the house and sell them for a bottle of wine, even if the article he took was of much greater value.

On one occasion, during a wet and heavy snowing winter's day, I was not able to go to school as my shoes were very old and had holes in the soles. Mother had no money to take the shoes to be repaired. Our "aunt," the wife of our mother's cousin who was a military man, was visiting us, and she asked why I was not in school. Mother replied that my shoes were letting water in, and in order not to catch a cold, she kept me home. Without saying anything, my aunt went to the city and bought me the best shoes on the market.

The next day I went to school, proud of my new shoes. I felt like the richest kid in the class, if not the entire school.

Unfortunately, a few days later I got a bad cold and had to stay in bed. After recovering I was ready to go back to school, but as I was getting dressed, I could not find my new shoes anywhere. I searched the whole house in vain.

Then a thought came to me. I recalled my father coming in the house for a short time. I was almost sure he had taken my shoes and had sold them for a drink, but the problem was to whom? There was a shoe repairer not far from our house who was a good shoemaker, but he also liked to drink. I knew my father often talked and drank with him. Did he sell my shoes to this man?

The best way for me to find out was to go to his workshop. As soon as I entered the shop, I saw my shoes on the shelf with a very high price tag on them. There was also a note saying "new shoes."

The master, as we called the tradesman, asked me what brought me to his shop. I told him that my shoes were very old and beyond repair, and I asked if he had some old shoes that were better than mine that he could sell me.

"Yes," he said, "I have just the shoes for you. Cheap enough for you to afford since that wicked father of yours does not care for you."

He told me the price and asked me to try them on. After trying them on, I told him they were a little tight. I then asked him if I could try the shoes with the tag that read "new shoes."

The Vacant Seat

"Don't you see the price? You could never afford them," he said.

But I pleaded, "Could I at least try them on to see how it feels to have new shoes on?"

Here he made a very fatal mistake. He gave me both shoes to try on. But I did not try them on. As soon as I had them in my hands, I ran as fast as I could with my shoes in my hands. He yelled after me, "Thief, thief!" But he could not catch up with me because I was the fastest runner in my class.

There were times when we were short of food. This happened when the winters were unusually long and cold and so, before the spring came and the new crops could be planted, we would run out of stock. We had to sparingly use the food we had in the cellar, such as potatoes, pumpkins, and carrots. When the corn in the barn ran out, we were in trouble because we depended on corn as a staple food.

On one particular day, our mother was promised help with food, but the help never came. And money she had lent to others in their time of need was not repaid. I can still vividly remember that particular evening when she told us, with tears in her eyes, that she could not prepare any meal for us and that we had to go to bed without any food. She then went on to tell us the Lord would take care of us and tomorrow would be better. I heard her telling us this with a heavy heart. Young as I was, I wondered how the Lord would take care of us if we did nothing about our situation. We often asked God for help, but at times the Lord seemed to not hear us, no matter how much we prayed.

In my young mind I decided the Lord wanted us to do something ourselves and very quickly. I knew I would have to do something.

One of my uncles was a communist, and he was rich. They lived a plentiful life and had food and clothing. But they had never offered to help our mother who was struggling to bring us up. When I heard her say we had to go to bed without food, I decided to do something about it. I decided I would go to my uncle and ask for money.

I knew my mother wouldn't allow me to do that, so I snuck out of the house and went to my uncle's house. He wasn't home, and my aunt was unfriendly, telling me he was at the pub with his friends. She said, "Don't you know that your uncle is a drunk and spends all the money on drink and does not care for his family?"

But I knew different, and I didn't accept her reasons. Yes, he did drink a lot, but he was also a caring father. They had two children, a son and a daughter. The son was nine years older than me, and the daughter was my age. She was my favorite cousin and remains so to this day, even though we now live worlds apart.

After my aunt told me he was in a pub, I decided to look for him. I had to find him if we were to have some food. I went to one of the drinking houses in the town. I felt strange for I had never been to such a place, and I admit I hated the people who owned these terrible places for that is where my father spent all his money instead of caring for us.

As I opened the door I could not see my uncle, so I went to another pub, and as soon as I opened the door, I saw my uncle drinking with his friends. At that moment my uncle turned his head and looked in my direction. He very excitedly called for me to come in, and as I entered he introduced me to his drinking friends.

"This is my brilliant nephew of whom I am very proud; he has the best grades at school!"

He then offered to buy me a soft drink, but I urged him to hear me out for I had something important to tell him in private. He finally stepped away from his friends and asked me what was the matter.

"Uncle, we have nothing to eat; we have no money to buy any food."

"What?" he said. "You have no money and no food? I am going to kill that ugly father of yours!"

Then I asked if he could give me some money, and without a word, he put his hand in his pocket and took out a handful of squashed paper money and put it into my waiting hand. As soon as I had that money, I thanked him and ran home as fast as I could. When I arrived home I showed the money to my mother, and when she counted it, she found that there was about three months salary of an average factory worker.

She could not believe that my uncle gave me all this money. She kept asking me if I had stolen it. With much assurance I finally convinced her that it was from my uncle, and with that assurance, she stopped urging me to take it back. I must confess that I don't think I would have taken it back at the time even if I had stolen it.

She gave some of the money to my older brother and told him to go to the baker and buy just one loaf of bread as the next day she would buy flour and make her own. However, my brother bought five loaves, saying he was so hungry he could eat two by himself. I noticed tears in my mother's eyes, but she said nothing.

My mother, Branka, Mira, and I suffered the most during our father's insanity, the only word I can think of to describe him at that time. He seemed to be driven by some force that gave him no peace, nor us. But during that whole time our mother had an unflinching faith in God. She never for a moment doubted that somehow, someday God would bring an end to the nightmare. I, on the other hand, felt that if God was in charge, what had we done to deserve this?

My friends had good families with caring fathers who made sure their children, despite very difficult postwar times, had at least the basic needs of life.

The heartaches of life seemed to surround me. My home situation was less than ideal and then my best friend died at the tender age of thirteen. His name was Milenko or Misha as we called him. He had a wonderful and kind grandfather, and since both of my grandparents were dead, his grandfather was like my own.

It was early Friday morning when my mother went to the markets to sell some of the produce from the garden. Before leaving my mother told me and my sisters to take the bread out of the oven, a large country oven she had built herself that could fit five big loaves of bread at a time.

The Vacant Seat

The same large ovens were also used as saunas. After the bread was taken out, people who suffered rheumatics would crawl in and stay inside long enough to sweat. I never dared to do this; to me it felt too dangerous, even though the fire was out.

Mother told me that I should also help my sisters around the house. At about 9:00 a.m. Misha arrived at our home with his sister and another friend from the neighborhood. He asked me to go swimming with them, but I told him I had to help my sisters. I told him that if he helped me do my chores then we could go together. He and the others were in a rush to get to the river, so they left. Sadly, the day ended in tragedy for my "brother," as we called each other, for he never came back.

It was a terrible loss not only for his loving family but for all of us, especially for me as a twelve year old, and it took me a long time to accept that he was no longer among the living.

After he died, I was left to beg for help from others. I recall how I had no pencil to write with and had to rely on the goodness of my friends who gave me their pencils when they were no longer able to use the three centimeter long sticks. For me though, that was like a new pencil. It was the same with exercise books. Some of my friends would tear a leaf out of their books and give it to me so I could write notes from the teacher's lectures. My cousins, due to their mother's dislike of our mother, did not help even though they were in a very good position to do so since my uncles were considered "rich" by the standards of that time.

Being a Christian, our mother taught us to bear all of these trials patiently. She also taught us that no matter how our father acted and how cruelly he treated us we should always show him respect and never utter a nasty or disrespectful word to him. I must admit, at that time I could not understand our mother's attitude.

Although we grew up under difficult circumstances, there were also many good times. There was no money to buy toys, but that did not stop us from playing with toys we made ourselves. Growing up in a farming community where people had horses and stables, we made "horses" from corncobs and our stables were made from mud, of which there was plenty since the roads were not paved. In summer it was a dirt-dust road, and in winter we played in the deep mud road, and that was our paradise. We could play for hours without becoming bored.

The only problem was when it was time to come inside. Our poor mother had her hands full cleaning us and washing the only clothes we had. Every wash time was also a bedtime since we had no change of clothes. To be naked and walk around was very shameful, so we had to go to bed whenever she washed our clothes. Winter was the most difficult time as we were forced to sleep in one room, which was usually the kitchen, for warmth.

Chapter 7

Eating Organic

It is interesting to note that nowadays people pay a lot of money to buy or grow organic food. Millions of dollars are spent on advertising organically produced food. But to us it was considered normal to eat such food. We were not even aware that we were eating healthy food.

We had our own garden that the communist leaders had allowed us to keep. We had approximately four acres, and we had to grow food for the whole year to last until the next season's crops were ready to harvest. Our mother also had many chickens, geese, ducks, and other domestic animals that produced food. She farmed pigs for food and also to sell. We also had at least one cow, some sheep, and goats for milk. We grew potatoes, onions, and cabbages for winter, as well as corn, wheat, and other grains—all on just four acres of land.

Along with other vegetables, we also grew watermelons, and I remember this very well because watermelons were seasonal fruit and could only be eaten in the summer, unlike today, when you can buy them generally year round in the supermarkets. We planted the watermelons in April or early May. We then had to wait three months for them to be ready to harvest and eat. All of our neighbors also grew watermelons, and as it happened, our next-door neighbor planted her watermelons earlier than our mother, resulting in her watermelons being bigger and ready to harvest earlier than our own.

We children, especially my older sister Branka, watched those lovely watermelons grow. We were very impatient and kept asking our mother as to when they would be ready to pick so we could eat them. In response she told us in rather strict tones not to touch them and that when they were ready she would pick them herself and only then could we have them. To us, it seemed a long way off, and we wondered if there was some other way that would enable us to taste the wonderfully delicious fruit a little earlier.

My sister and I thought rather hard as to how to achieve our plan, and every day for about a week we looked at our mother's biggest watermelon and at our next-door neighbor's melons. Our neighbor's watermelon was much bigger, and to our understanding, it was overdue for picking. Every time we thought about the juicy fruit, our mouths would water. But how could we get it? We had no money to buy it, and we were sure the good neighbor would not negotiate a sale anyway. But we wanted the watermelon.

So my sister and I made a pact; we would get it and we would eat it. The decision was made, and we proceeded to put it into practice. Of course it was to be top secret. Truth was, we were about to become thieves.

Whether it was my sister or I who was the first to suggest this "grand plan" I cannot remember, but making sure no one saw us, we went to our neighbor's garden where there were no fences, grabbed the huge and extremely heavy watermelon, and without missing a step, ran into our mother's crop of high corn.

The Vacant Seat

Here, we felt safe.

We were sure no one saw us and since we had no knife or fork, nor a plate to serve on, we just dropped the watermelon on the ground. As it broke the glorious red flesh of the fruit stared at us like bright sunshine. We sat on the ground and started eating as a lion with its prey. Oh it was sweet, so very sweet.

We didn't speak. We had no time. We just ate and ate until it was finished. Then suddenly, we heard a noise that sounded like someone walking through the corn. We were sure no one had seen us, yet the noise came closer and closer. At this stage we hoped a cloud would come hide us, but as the noise became louder and louder, the awful realization hit us hard—someone had discovered our terrible deed.

We sat quietly hoping not to be found. Then the rustling stopped, and we saw two feet—the feet were familiar; they belonged to our mother!

We dared not look up, nor did we utter a word. She was kind and wonderful, but she could also be very firm. We awaited her wrath.

"Is the watermelon sweet?" she asked.

What answer could we give? Until now it had been sweet, but now there was no answer, and the downfall of Adam and Eve came back to haunt us, and we began blaming and accusing each other.

"He told me to do that!"

"No, she told me to do that."

Our wise mother asked no further questions.

"Pick up the pieces and come with me," she said.

We were filthy and wet, and the pieces were full of soil. But we picked them up and followed her through the corn. We could have run, but we knew better than that.

To go back to our house, we would have followed the path through the garden straight toward our home. To go to our neighbor, we had to turn to the left after we got out of the cornfield. To our horror, this is exactly what our mother did. She turned to the left and made sure we followed. We were hoping we would be punished with a spanking, but now we were scared.

When we reached the back door of our neighbor's house, mother knocked. Soon the kind lady opened the door. She was somewhat surprised to see us so filthy, and she seemed equally surprised to see the filthy pieces of watermelon.

"Yes, my dear neighbor, what is the news?" she asked our mother.

"Do you have watermelons in your garden?" our mother asked.

"Yes, I do," was the reply.

"Well from now on you will have to guard your watermelons, for you have thieves next door who are stealing your watermelons, and these are the thieves," mother said, pointing to us.

That was the greatest and best form of punishment, one that at the time we could not understand, but as we grew older we came to realize the wisdom behind it.

Never again did we steal anything, particularly watermelons.

Our dear mother had taught us one of the many realities of life. A lesson my sister and I never forgot.

Chapter 8

The Church

It was by coincidence our mother met a family who were members of a little known Christian church.

How our mother came in contact with them I have never found out, but always willing to help those in worse conditions, she offered for them to live in our house in the vineyard rent-free since they had no home, and they gladly accepted the offer. In return they were to help us tend the vineyard, which was a good arrangement that kept both families happy.

Seeing their poverty, our mother took some cooking utensils and some "good" food to the family. She prepared chicken, duck, and some pork. She also made some cakes and cooked vegetables. The lady was very grateful for the help, but when she saw the meat our mother had prepared, the lady promptly refused to accept them.

"Are you sick and not allowed to eat meat?" asked mother. "At least give it to the children," she entreated.

"No, we are not sick. On the contrary, we are all very healthy, but we are vegetarians."

"Vegetarians?" This was news to our mother. "Why are you vegetarians?"

She knew Jewish people ate only "clean" meat and never used pork, but no meat at all was rather strange. The woman explained that they belonged to a church that promoted vegetarianism as a good way of live. To our mother, at that time, this was not acceptable. However, she showed keen interest in what the woman had to say about other aspects of her faith.

As time went on, not only did our mother become interested in this "new faith," but it also had a profound impact on me. By now I knew Communism was failing. George had joined "The Party," as they called it, and he strongly urged me to follow him by joining as well. Predrag refused to be drawn into any party or faith. He just wanted to become rich, to have the money he never had as a child. That was his purpose, and he eventually achieved this goal.

My main goal, on the other hand, was to achieve higher education, although how I would do that I did not know.

I had also refused to be drawn into the communist philosophy, which might have had good theories but at the same time oppressed all those who would not see things the same way as the communists did.

The world had just experienced the most horrific time in history under the monstrous rule of Adolf Hitler, and now the communists who were promising freedom and prosperity to all had demonstrated different policies.

The Vacant Seat

My mother had a little Bible she often read. I asked if I could read it, and she was happy to let me, but she warned me to be very careful should father come home as he would not like it and would be very angry.

One day my mother had to go attend to some work, as was usually the case, and I was left at home by myself. I had no idea where the others were, but seeing I was by myself, I took the little Bible and started reading it. It just happened that as I started reading my father arrived. Being always antagonistic toward me and still refusing to accept me as his son, by now I was about thirteen year of age, he asked me what book I was reading. I told him simply that it was a "good book."

"Give it to me," he ordered.

This was a test of respect and loyalty to my mother. But on his insistence, I handed him the Bible. He grabbed it from me and walked toward our wood chopping shed. Once there he put the Bible on the chopping block, took a big axe, and sliced the Bible in half. He then walked to the well where we drew our drinking water and threw my mother's precious book down the well. His mission accomplished, he walked away.

I don't know if this was an act against my mother or me; it may have been both. I couldn't just leave the Bible in the deep, narrow, and dark well, so I lowered the bucket, which was tied to a chain, and after many attempts, I fished the Bible out in the bucket. It was a triumph over evil intent.

When mother arrived home, I showed her the Bible, telling her what had happened. Without any comment, tears began streaming down her face. Seeing my mother like that left a lasting impression upon my mind.

After seriously considering my future, I decided to look into the little known church that I now knew my mother was a member of. At this time I was in high school, and as I found out more about the church, which kept Saturday as a day of rest, I stopped going to school on Saturdays in order to keep God's holy law. At the time school was compulsory from Monday to Saturday, leaving Sunday as a day at home, even though the government was atheist.

This action provoked the anger of George and my uncles, who were by now in high leading positions in the government (one of my uncles eventually became president of Yugoslavia).

They offered me inducements in order to turn me away from what they called "your mother's fanatical religion," but at the same time they acknowledged that this was the best way for her to survive the hell she had been forced to endure.

Uncle Steven tried his best to persuade me to reject this religion. He claimed it was for old people and not for the young. On one hand he was right because under the system of the Communist party it was impossible for a young person to achieve their goals and at the same time follow their religious beliefs.

The greatest pressure put on me, however, was by the school faculty. Until I began attending church, I had many friends at school, and I took active part in school activities. But when I stopped going to school on Saturdays, most of my friends rejected me. They also mocked and derided me with fierceness, something I never imagined would come from my closest friends.

The Church

Every day they would yell at me, "Sabbather! Sabbather!" They also called me all sorts of obscene names. The pressure grew stronger and stronger until the school board decided to expel me, regardless of my high grades. They made their decision on January 17, 1954. The decision (a document I have kept all this time) was read in front of each class, and when it was read in my class, the teacher told me, "Jaksic, pack your bags and go home!"

The document stated that it should serve as a warning to other students should they contemplate becoming a Sabbathkeeper.

The day after my expulsion Uncle Steven sent me a telegram and asked me to come see him immediately. He liked me very much and had even told me he loved me as much as his own son, who was three years younger. To refuse his invitation would have been offensive, so I went the next day. Despite his heavy schedule, he spent all day with me and offered for me to come live with him. If I accepted, he promised to fully support me financially and put me through school, something I very much desired. His son, not only my cousin but also my friend, also urged me to accept his father's offer.

It was a very difficult decision for me to make. Eventually, however, I came to the realization that there was something of much more value than everything my uncle was offering. Freedom. Being free from the human inventions and so-called solutions, which had no real answer.

I finally had to tell my uncle of my decision—I could not give up my faith in God and the teachings of the Bible, which I'd come to recognize as the Word of God. I thanked him very much for his kindness and his very generous offer, but I told him I could not do otherwise. He was speechless, to say the least. During supper he kept quiet, and there was an unbearable tension around the table. Soon after, I decided to go home. As we said goodbye, he wished me much success in my future.

After that meeting, I decided that I needed to leave the country. I could stay no longer. But first I knew I had to study something—"have something in my hands." My mother, admittedly, was also very concerned about my future.

My two older brothers were on their way to obtaining qualifications to bring them security, while my oldest sister was apprenticed with the best dressmaker in town, and her future was assured. My younger sister Mira was still in school, and our mother had arranged with another dressmaker in town for her to learn the trade after she finished school. And Beba was still very young with many years ahead of her at school. Thus, my future was a great cause for concern.

Sensing my mother's concern, I decided it was time to do something about my situation. In our village there were two private tailors. One of them was married to a distant relative, although I am still not sure whether she was related to my mother or my father. We called her Aunt Verica.

On one occasion her husband made me a pair of trousers, and after he notified us the trousers were finished, I brought them home, put them on, and found that they were about two sizes too big. But we didn't complain. I wore them with a string tied around my waste—belts were only worn by people who had money and who could afford to buy them.

The Vacant Seat

How my mother was able to obtain material and pay for the trousers is still a mystery to me. Of course, when my friends saw me in those trousers, they laughed and told me I should work in a circus as a clown. I didn't let that bother me though, by now I was used to such treatment. And these were the first tailor-made trousers I had ever owned. I was about fifteen years of age. Until then, my mother had always made my clothes.

When I went to school, I would always walk past my distant relative's shop. After I had been expelled, I decided to ask him to take me on as an apprentice, to teach me tailoring. Without even telling my mother, I walked into his shop and told him my reason for being there.

He told me no. "You should be going for a higher education. It is that religion that stopped you."

By now most people in the village knew why I was no longer in school.

Then he added, "No, I could not take you because you do not work on Saturdays, and we are busiest on Saturdays, finishing the garments for people to wear on Sunday."

His wife, who was in the back room, came to the front and told her husband to take me after our conversation ended. "He is a good boy; he will work hard," she said.

That surprised me. Firstly, I was not sure I was known as a "good boy," and secondly for the simple fact she had intervened on my behalf.

After some negotiations and giving me some almost impossible conditions to which I had to agree, he accepted me. I virtually ran home to tell the good news to my worrying mother. When she heard the news, she appeared somewhat perplexed and concerned. Noticing her worried face, I asked what was the matter.

She responded by telling me the tailor was sometimes a cruel and difficult man. But at the time, that didn't matter to me. What mattered is that I had a job.

But it was not long after commencing my training that the signs of what my mother had warned me about started to show in his attitude. He was indeed mean and cruel. On many occasions it got so bad that his wife had to intervene on my behalf.

Fortunately for me this situation did not last too long.

My oldest sister Bianka was by now living in Belgrade and working for the Seventh-day Adventist Reform Movement Church, of which she and my mother were now members. Four years later I also become a member. She managed to obtain training in typing and shorthand writing, thanks to a distant relative. The relatives who helped my sister had a personal tailor who had graduated in Paris in 1938, the year I was born.

My sister asked our relatives to ask this tailor if I could finish my apprenticeship with him, and in addition, since I too was a Sabbathkeeper, he was to give me Sabbath off. It worked well. The tailor agreed, and I went to live in Belgrade and work for him.

Chapter 9

Another Sabbath Test

When I was in Belgrade, I worked for the famous tailor Ljuba Filipovich. He gave me Sabbaths off, and things went well for a while. However, the winter came and the days became shorter. Since Sabbath starts at sunset, it meant I had to leave work earlier.

The test came one particular Friday when he gave me a job and told me to finish it before leaving. I had one hour, and I worked as fast as I could, but despite all my efforts to complete it, I could not. I kept delaying my leaving until I realized I had to go, giving myself a very short time to be ready for Sabbath, which involved personal preparation, such as shaving and showering and changing my clothes, before heading to the church for the Friday evening service. I finally told my "master" I had to go.

He responded very angrily by saying, "No! You cannot go yet. I gave you Saturday off, not Friday also."

He knew about my belief, but this time he refused to give in. It left me with very little choice. I had to go. I left my job unfinished and told him I was leaving. As I walked out of the workshop, he called out, "Do not come back. I do not want you anymore!"

I ran all the way home, arriving just in time to finish my Sabbath preparations in a hurry. The weekend was filled with joy and, at the same time, worry. On Monday morning I went to work and asked my boss what I should do.

But he responded, "There is no more work for you. Nothing. I told you not to come back; go away."

I had no option but to leave.

In order to not upset my mother and sister, I went to the city and spent time in the park before going home at the same time I would normally arrive after work.

My sister was happy to see me and asked me how my day was. I told her it was okay.

The next day I went back to work. I asked the same question "What shall I do?"

I got the same reply. This went on for three days, but on the fourth day, things changed.

As I appeared at work and asked my boss "What shall I do?" he calmly gave me work. That was the end of our confrontation. Never again did he try to stop me from leaving when I had to go. After completing my apprenticeship, I worked another seven months for him. While still working for him, Branka married his assistant, Peter Angelkovich, a highly qualified tailor in his own right.

More than three years after my expulsion from school, I still dreamed of leaving the country. But according to Yugoslavian law, at the age of seventeen I had to enter pre-military training, provided I was mentally and physically healthy. I passed the test and was sent to training. It was late autumn in 1955,

The Vacant Seat

and I was in a military camp of 400 people, all of whom were seventeen years old.

Training consisted of exercises, theory of defending our country, how to use a gun, how to defend ourselves from the enemy, and so on. However, with Yugoslavia being a Communist/atheist state, the military officers also engaged in antireligious propaganda. During these lectures against religion, all 400 of us would be ordered to stand in rows of fifty while one of the officers addressed us.

"That terrible book, the Bible," he would say, adding that religion was the invention of the poor and weak of mind and that the Bible was a book of inventions and fairy tales designed to keep people in fear.

After an hour of his talk on the "facts" of religion, he challenged anyone who was reading the "terrible book, the Bible" to come forward.

At first no one responded. But he repeated his challenge.

A friend of mine, also a believer and to whom I'd been talking to about the Bible asked me if I was going to go forward. I said yes, but he urged me not to, saying, "Who knows what they will do to you."

But I had to make a stand. This officer was challenging God and the Bible. I slowly started moving toward the front. Of the 400 people assembled, only three of us went forward.

The officer was very angry indeed. I'm not sure he expected anyone to dare come forward, and now that we had, he felt challenged. He briefly questioned the first two. After they gave him answers as to why they read the Bible, he turned them around and kicked them as hard as he could with his heavy boots before sending them back in line.

Then came my turn. By now he was so enraged his face was all scrunched up, and he had an evil look that proved he was very angry indeed.

Then he asked me, "And why do you read the Bible?"

With a clear and loud voice, I told him, "I read the Bible because the Bible tells me about Jesus Christ my Savior."

This response was too much for his communist/atheist beliefs, and he told me, "And now I am going to see if Jesus Christ your Savior can save you from my hands."

With absolute rage he started beating me mercilessly. He kicked me with his heavy boots, punched me with his fists, and then threw me to the ground and continued hitting me and stomping on me.

Physically, although healthy, I was thin, and at first I felt the painful blows, but after a while, somehow I lost all feeling, and his blows had little effect on me. Before passing out I yelled as loud as I could with my now weak voice, "I will stop reading the Bible only when you kill me!"

He probably would have killed me if it hadn't been for two officers who intervened to save me from this mad man. I came to as I felt them dragging me from the platform. They took me to a small room where I lay on the floor for a long time. After I recovered, I made my mind up to not only continue to read the Bible but to become a fully-fledged follower of Christ.

The communist theories of brotherhood and equality of all and prosperity now meant nothing to me. That was, indeed, only a fairy tale, and an evil one at that.

After my full recovery, I went back to work with new determination to be Christian and to leave Yugoslavia as soon as possible.

Chapter 10

First Move to Leave

It wasn't easy to obtain a passport unless you had finished your military service, which was usually two years.

I had read in the daily papers about an international horticultural show in Kolon, Germany. To attend, you had to be a member of the horticultural society of Yugoslavia. To my surprise, it was easy to become a member, and I soon received my green membership card. With the card in hand, I went to the travel agency and requested a ticket to Germany.

This part was not as easy as I had thought. Not being experienced in international travel (I was just over seventeen years old), I was told that I could go, but before I went, I had to have a passport. They told me I had to get the passport and then return to them for my travel documents.

I thought it wouldn't be a problem since my uncle was an important official in the government, and because he had power, I thought he would be able to help me get the passport. Not losing any time, I called my uncle. His wife answered, and as always, when she heard my voice, she was very friendly, asking me how I was doing. I told her I was okay, but that I needed to see my uncle regarding an important matter.

She asked if I could tell her what the matter was, so I told her my plan to travel to Germany and my need of a passport. Her reply was encouraging, and she indicated that she was sure my uncle would help me but that he was sick and in bed. However, she told me come to the house to see him.

Upon arrival she took me to the bedroom where my uncle was lying in bed. He looked extremely sick. (He was suffering from a liver problem that would eventually kill him.) When he saw me he was very happy I was there. I too was glad to see him, as it had been over a year since I'd seen him last.

After the preliminaries, I told him my travel plans and that I needed a passport. I then asked him if he could help me obtain it. He replied in a very kind way, but he was still very firm.

"No," he said, "I cannot help you. The law says that you must first finish your military duty. After you finish serving in the army, if you still wish to travel, come see me, and I will help you with a passport. And not only that, I will give you money to travel. I will pay your expenses to go abroad."

I could see there were no negotiations. I had lunch with my aunty, wished my uncle well, and said goodbye.

The Vacant Seat

I had a friend whose father had connections with people who were helping others leave the country, so I contacted my friend and asked him the details. He told me his father could help me and added that he, too, wanted to leave. He suggested we go together.

We were to go by train as kitchen hands, and as we approached the border, we would be hidden in a food storage section. It, of course, would cost some money.

As we made arrangements for this and were about to board the train for Germany, my friend's father came to us and said the people involved in this business had been caught and imprisoned. Fortunately, we did not lose any money as the arrangement had been to pay on the train.

Both plans to leave the country had failed, so I had to think about some other options. The only way to escape now was to go on foot at night and cross the border to Italy.

My plan was to travel to the city nearest the border and then walk at night to the border over the mountains. One of our church members and his wife, along with their one-year-old daughter, had the same plan as they, too, had been denied a passport. We agreed to go together.

We made a plan to travel by train as far as possible and then by bus to the town nearest the border. The plan worked well, and we reached the tourist city of Koper in Slovenia (which was then a state of Yugoslavia). After resting for two days, early in the evening of August 23, 1957, we started our walk toward the Italian border.

We were well-equipped with food and clothing to climb the high and rough mountains. It was a very dark and cloudy night, and a light rain fell. We had our maps, and although we were not sure of the terrain or the exact area where the border was, we kept climbing. It was difficult as we had to carry the child and the child's mother who was a rather large lady. Many times we had to stop and rest. We were wet and dirty, and we started feeling tired. But the thought of reaching the land of freedom gave us the energy to keep going.

We were almost on the summit when my friend told me to stay with his wife and child while he scouted out the summit. He returned and was very excited. When we reached the top of the mountain, in front of us were the city lights of Trieste, illuminating the whole sky. Although not exactly sure where the border was, we knew it was not far.

At this stage, though, we were not aware of what lay ahead.

We started descending the mountain. After about an hour, we came across a small path, and thinking we had crossed the border, we started talking loud—we were excited we had made it through so easily. For some reason, I was not so sure, and a kind of fear came upon me. The longer we walked, the more anxious I became.

I told the couple we should get off the path and go straight down toward the city, through the scrub brush. They assured me we were on the right track and said there was nothing to fear.

Just ten minutes after my warning, we were shocked when a huge German shepherd jumped out of the scrub and, roaring as a lion, circled around us. We immediately stopped. If we hadn't, the huge animal would likely have torn us to pieces. Seconds later two heavily armed soldiers with machine guns pointed at us ordered us to walk ten steps backward. Then they ordered us to lie on our stomachs and put our hands on our backs. As we did that, before approaching, they asked if we were armed with weapons of any kind. After assuring them we had nothing, they handcuffed all three of us.

At this moment my mind went completely blank. I had no idea what was happening to us. It was like a bad nightmare.

The soldiers got us up and directed us to walk to their camp. With due respect to them, the soldiers were polite, very efficient, and did not treat us cruelly.

After arriving an officer came and told us we had been caught in a prohibited area, but he would wait until morning to question us. Until then, we were to stay in the lock up. They offered us food and milk for the baby.

That night I could not sleep. I don't think that any of us slept, except the baby, who was unaware of the dire situation we were in. Before leaving for this journey, I thought if I believed, prayed, and fasted God would hear me and my plans would succeed. This was something I had firmly believed.

If someone had suggested to me God would allow us to be caught on the border, I would have told them, "Get behind me, Satan."

Now as I was sitting handcuffed as a prisoner, a voice kept telling me, "Where is your God now? You rejected all the wonderful offers of your uncle. You gave up your good prospects for your future. You thought God would give you a miracle and take you on some kind of wings to a better land."

These thoughts tortured me, and I tried to dispel them, but they persisted. Right at that moment, I could have been in my dear uncle's home enjoying the comfort and the privileges a nephew of a great leader. But instead, I was a prisoner, regarded as a criminal. I wondered what lay ahead for me. What was my future now? If only I'd listened to my uncle, but it was too late.

When morning finally arrived, a high ranking officer came to our room and told us that because we were caught trying to cross the border illegally, we would be interrogated, and depending on our answers, we would be charged with spying against the country, something which carried a severe penalty of many years in prison or even death in some cases. He then took us to the office where we were to be questioned.

Before the interrogation started, they separated me from my friends, and to our surprise, they let my friend's wife go back home. This sounded too good to be true, but it was.

Then the humiliating interrogation started. They told me that as I was caught entering Yugoslavia illegally and was being charged with spying against the country. They wanted to know where I was from and who my contacts were.

The Vacant Seat

I was shocked to hear that we were "entering" Yugoslavia. And I was upset because if my friends had taken notice of my pleadings and gone straight down toward Trieste, we would not be here.

The interrogator demanded answers. I told him we were not spies, we were not in the "west," and we met no one. But he didn't believe me. He raised his voice and shouted at me from the top of his voice, "You are a traitor, and you will pay for this!"

He then told me that my friend had confessed everything and that if I did not confess I would receive a much greater penalty. After a few hours of this mind torture, he took me to a small room and locked me up. By now I was very hungry, thirsty, and tired. No one came for hours.

Then as night was approaching, an officer came and told me I was going to be transported to another prison. Without giving me any food or water, I was handcuffed to a police officer and led to the train station. As we entered the train, people stared at me, some stuck out their tongues, and others yelled, "Serves you right, you criminal, whatever you have done." Some elderly women were even saying, "So young and already a criminal. He needs to be well punished to learn his lesson."

As the train started moving, I felt tired and sleepy, but each time I dosed off the police officer would prod me in my ribs, not allowing me to sleep. That was shear torture, not only to my mind but also to my body, which I felt would give up. I was so weary yet was not allowed any sleep.

We finally arrived to our destination, and the officer took me to the prison. This prison was like a torture chamber—a small cell that could accommodate up to ten people at most. Yet there were more than twenty of us inside. There were no beds, no toilets, no washing facilities, no windows, and only a very faint electric lamp, so it was almost completely dark.

As the police officer roughly pushed me inside, the prisoners, the sorry looking sub-humans, were startled. Most of them were in their forties or fifties. No one talked. They all were standing since there were no chairs or beds. I noticed boards leaning against the walls, and I asked where the beds were. They told me the boards were the beds.

"But you cannot lie down. You have to lean on those boards and sleep standing up, leaning against them."

The worst of all was the lack of air. There was no window, only a kind of grill at the top of the iron door. From time to time the grill would be opened briefly to let air in, and then closed again. The prisoners would start banging on the iron door and screaming at the top of their weakened bodies, "Air, air, air." They would bang on the door with their fists and legs and would curse until air was let in.

This continued twenty-four hours a day, every day.

We were hungry and thirsty. Each of us received about half a kilogram of bread a day and about half a liter of water. When you finished with that, you had to wait until the next day to receive more.

The toilet was a forty-four-gallon drum cut in half with a sharp top. Everyone had to relieve themselves in there. The stench was unbearable as it was only emptied every second or third day. The inmates kept asking me what crime I had committed to be thrown in there.

I told them I was a Christian and that is why I was there. They laughed at me and didn't believe my story. Then they asked me if I knew where I was. I answered that I was in prison, and they said, "Oh, that is true, you are in prison, but do you know what kind of prison you are in?"

This puzzled me, and I asked them what kind of prison it was. The answer shocked me.

"Death row cell," they responsed. "People do not stay here long, ten to fifteen days. After that they are called out and shot dead, executed about ten meters from the cell door. We hear each execution. You will hear when the next person is called. After a few minutes you will hear the gunshots."

I did not know what to think. I had not been tried by a court. I had not been sentenced to death. Why was I here? This perplexed me, but for some reason I was not afraid. I thought that if God wanted me to die then there was nothing I could do.

As I waited, I noticed that the walls of the cell were old and had never been painted. They were of grey cement. I found a piece of rock and started writing on the wall. I wrote texts from the Bible such as John 3:16, portions of the Ten Commandments, and others that told about God's love and forgiveness and the promise of eternal life.

The prisoners watched me with great interest, but no one said anything. And what was more surprising, the guards did not stop me. The walls of the cell were now my Bible, and every morning and night I read a text.

I thanked the Lord that I had read the Word of God, and now in my darkest hour, and in the darkest hour of these poor human beings, we could all read about a better tomorrow.

Chapter 11

The Second Attempt

As the days progressed, I found out that most of the men were political prisoners who had opposed the government or been involved in some plot against the government, which was why they had been sentenced to death.

Among them was a man who was unable to stand or even sit. He lay on the floor; his face was very swollen, obviously from beatings. No one spoke to him, nor did he speak to anyone. For some reason I felt I should talk to him, so I went to him and asked what had happened and why they had mutilated him so badly.

At first he told me to go away and not to speak to him, but I felt compelled to talk to him, and finally after many attempts he responded. He told me he had killed his wife who was a high ranking communist leader. I asked him why he would do such a terrible deed, and he told me his whole story.

One day he had arrived home from work early and found his wife in bed with another man. He took out his revolver and tried to shoot the man. However, the man escaped through the window. He shot his wife, and then fled to a neighboring country, for he lived near the border. After living there for some years, one night there was a knock on his door. When he opened it, two men grabbed him and brought him back to Yugoslavia. He was tried and sentenced to death.

"I am here," he told me, "not for killing my wife, but for killing a communist."

I then told him I was a Christian. I told him about the love of God and the promise of eternal life. I told him that if he was to repent with all his heart, God would forgive him. I told him that even if he was put to death, when Christ comes He will raise him from the dead and give him life eternal.

The man was startled to say the least. He asked me very surprisingly, "Do you really believe this?"

I assured him that I did, and I told him that you could believe as well. For the next few days we talked about the love of God and eternal life. Prior to talking to this man and also prior to writing the texts on the wall, I was very perplexed and felt uncertain about my relationship with God. But now I understood why God had allowed me to come to this dreadful place. It was for this man. This man had to hear the gospel, the good news. I was at peace.

After about ten days, my name was called. As I gathered my few belongings, the poor man I'd led to God grabbed me and wept. He told me to pray for him and never to forget him. I never have.

The Second Attempt

After that I was transported to another prison, and another, until I was brought to the city of Novi Sad where I was interrogated by a cruel and sadistic man. He wanted me to confess and tell him which western country I was spying for. Despite my total denial that I was working for any western country, he kept threatening and assaulting me. Finally, when he saw that all his efforts to force some kind of confession from me hadn't worked, he tried another tactic. He insinuated I was mentally disturbed and asked me if I knew where I was. I told him I knew I was in central UDBA—the Yugoslav secret police.

"Oh," he responded, "You are intelligent. You know that there is UDBA."

When he told me I was intelligent, I decided to play his game. In the office where I was being interrogated, through the window I could clearly see parliament house where my uncle was the president.

Without waiting for him to say more mocking words to me, I continued, "And I know this is the White House."

"What is this white house?" he asked.

I replied, "This is the people's assembly."

"Oh," he continued, mocking me, "You are more clever then I thought."

But again I went on, "And I know someone who works there. He is my uncle."

"Hey," he sounded very surprised. "And what is he doing? Is he cleaning windows?"

"Perhaps he sometimes cleans windows," I replied.

"And tell me, what is his name?"

This was the moment I was praying and waiting for. I knew very well the communists feared each other and the higher in the government the higher the power and authority they had. So I told him my uncle's name.

Until this moment, the man had been acting so powerful, as if he was some sort of god. Now he became pale and was left speechless for a few moments. I watched his face very intently to see his reaction.

After a few moments he gathered some composure and then again, threatening me, said he was going to leave me alone in the room to think about my confession and to admit that I was spying on the country. He said that when he returned, if I still did not admit to my crime, he would break my head with the heavy glass ashtray on the corner of his desk.

I did not say anything, but my thoughts were, You will do nothing of the sort; you are finished.

As it happened, he knew my uncle personally, so he called him. When he told my uncle he was interrogating me as a possible spy against the country, my uncle, without commenting on the allegations against me, told him to let me go immediately. He confirmed he knew me and told him not to treat me the way they treat the enemies of the people.

When he returned, he was a different man. He did not tell me he had spoken to my uncle, but he told me that seeing as I was a very stubborn young man, he had decided to let me go. Then he added, "This is not the end; you will be tried in court."

The Vacant Seat

Then he told me he had arranged for my clothes to be brought to the office, stating I did not have to go back to prison. When my clothes arrived, I changed and left my prison garb on the floor. Then I left.

It was September 1957, and as I got out, it was still very hot. I was weak after four months of hardly any food, so much so that I could barely walk. I felt faint and had to sit down on the ground every few steps. It was a Saturday, so I decided to go to church where I could rest. It took a long time for me to find the church. Even though I knew the city quite well, I'd never had to walk from the prison.

Finally, after a torturous walk in the heat for about two hours, I knew where I was. When I finally arrived, the people there were surprised and shocked to see me, particularly in the condition I was in. They were very kind and provided me with a shower, a change of clothes, and best of all, good food, food I had not eaten during the whole ordeal. And there was plenty of it.

After resting there for two days, I went home to my village. When my mother saw me, she was so overwhelmed she embraced me and cried uncontrollably. Finally she told me that before leaving I should have told her my plans, and she would have prayed for me. "For the Lord hears the prayers of faithful mothers," she said.

I also strongly believed that, but I hadn't told her because I had been worried she would hold me back.

After a few days of rest, I went back to work. To my surprise, my boss took me back without question, although he told me the police had told him I was in prison on the charges of spying. He did not believe their story and encouraged me to leave the country as soon as I could. He was also against the system, but could do nothing himself as he had the business and was married with two children.

He had belonged to a secret organization opposing the government, but they didn't engage in public demonstrations or any subversive activities. They worked in a silent manner, spreading their philosophy wherever they could. He asked me to arrange a meeting with my uncle, but my uncle declined to meet with him. That indicated to me the government knew of their existence but did nothing to suppress it.

I continued to work in Belgrade for another year before deciding to make another attempt to leave the country. All efforts to gain a passport failed. The only option was to again attempt to escape over the mountains.

This time I went with my close friend Joseph. We were like blood brothers and were in the same situation with the military experience. We traveled much the same way as I had with my other friend and his wife and child, who had by now given up the idea of leaving the country.

Joseph and I traveled north to Koper. We spent a few days sightseeing, and then we made our way toward the border. The Lord said no again, and we were caught. For me it seemed much worse a situation as it was my second time, but Joe was indeed a friend and took it upon himself to take the blame for our attempt to leave the country illegally. We were separated, and he was sent to his hometown and sentenced to six months in prison.

I, on the other hand, was to be publicly humiliated. They handcuffed me to a police officer and led me through the streets of the tourist city to show what happens to those who try to leave the country illegally. As I was led around the streets, there was a lot of yelling, and I am sure some people would have torn me to shreds if it wasn't for the burly police officer holding me. People spat at me, threw rocks, made rude gestures, and much more. However, I seemed to be in some kind of tranquility, as though it was not me who was going through the ordeal and that I too was watching the poor young man being exposed to such terrible humiliation.

After about three to four hours of walking, the police officer took me to a cell. The walk had its benefits because as I was being led around the streets I forgot about myself. I busied myself reading the shop signs, and I saw a large sign advertising a clothing shop. The name of the proprietor was one I recognized. It was the same name a friend had given me, telling me if I should ever want to work there I should ask this man. I memorized the name and formed a new plan, a new strategy I felt would work.

As soon as I was released, I planned to write to this man to ask him for a job. That way I felt I would have a better chance to succeed in my escape. I was released after about four months, again with the help of my uncle who was very patient and never gave up on me, but my uncle gave me a stern warning that there would be no more rescuing. He informed me of a new law put in place that all those attempting to leave the country illegally would have one chance to "stop" at the shout of soldiers, and if they refused to stop, they would be killed.

The victims would then be buried, fully clothed, with no clue as to their identity; thus their relatives would never know whether their loved ones were successful or whether they had been killed in the attempt.

He gave this warning to my dear mother as well, and she urged me not to try again. It was now September 1958.

Chapter 12

The Third Attempt

After being released I spent a short time at home resting. During this time period, I wrote a letter to George who lived north on the coast of the Adriatic Sea.

Being a civil engineer, he was in charge of the construction of a multistory international hotel on the island of St. Catherine, not far from the mainland. I wrote to him and asked if I could spend some time with him and his family. I clearly needed to recuperate from my ordeal in prison. He said I was welcome to come and stay as long as I needed to, so I took the opportunity.

My brother and his wife, Cathy, received me with open arms. At that time they had a young son, and I had a wonderful time with them, but after a month I decided I should move on. I wrote a letter to the tailor in Koper where I had been led through the streets. To my pleasant surprise, he replied to come immediately, so the next day I booked a ticket to go by boat.

The trip took seven hours, and as I traveled, my greatest concern was that I had already been in the city twice, both times after being caught at the border and the second time being taken through town and humiliated. Now I was planning to work there and stay for at least a month, with the end goal of getting to know the border.

As I journeyed along the calm Adriatic Sea, I was unable to enjoy the beautiful coastal scenery because of the dread I was anticipating upon arrival to the city where I had been captured and humiliated. Finally, the boat arrived, and we prepared to disembark. As I walked off the boat toward the pier, I saw a man looking at me, and as I came closer, he walked toward me and asked simply, "Tailor?"

I responded yes, and he introduced himself as Ivan. After shaking hands, he told me we would go to his home where his wife had prepared a room for me.

"You will be staying with us."

He seemed rather happy to have help for his business. At that time the communist government allowed small enterprises and private businesses four workers and four apprentices. Since I had graduated, I would work as a tailor, and he would then employ an apprentice who would be assigned to me to teach. It was a good system as far as teaching young people trades.

After arriving at his house, I noticed that his wife was much younger than him, and they had two small children. I also noticed he was walking with a limp. I later learned he had lost his leg in the Second

The Third Attempt

World War. I also learned he was a member of the communist party. That did not concern me since most of my relatives, including George, were party members.

In the evening before I went to sleep, he told me he would employ me for a two-week trial period, and if all went okay, he would keep me. Otherwise we would part company. I told him that was okay with me. That night I did not sleep much; instead, I prayed and hoped that everything would go well. I was not sure what his expectations were but assumed they would be high, as in my letter to him I had stated I trained with a very reputable Belgrade tailor who got his diploma in Paris.

His wife gave me breakfast, and we then walked to the workshop, which was a block from their home. Upon entering he introduced me to all his workers, and I noticed that there were more people then allowed by the government. He told me they were casuals and that he was allowed to keep some part-time workers. Communists, as I have mentioned before, always operated under some level of fear and always had to justify their actions. I was a little apprehensive and unsure of the job he wanted me to do. He showed me the machine I would work at and gave me a spring coat to work on, which he had cut the previous day. He said most jobs were done by machine, not by hand.

I was familiar with this type of work, which was good, so I started working on it, only stopping for the morning and lunch breaks. I had never made a coat like that in one day, but that day I completed it.

When all the people had left, he came to me and asked how I was doing. I told him I thought it was okay and showed him the coat. He could not believe I had finished it completely and asked me to go with him to a milk bar.

In those days most transactions and agreements were done in milk bars where one could order coffee or other non-alcoholic drinks. As we sat down, he asked me if I would like coffee, but I told him I didn't drink coffee. He then offered me a cigarette, which I also declined. He seemed surprised to meet a young man who didn't drink coffee or smoke.

I told him a glass of milk would be fine, and he told me he was going to keep me—there was no need to wait two weeks.

He asked me how much I wanted to be paid. In private enterprises one had to negotiate pay, while in the government institutions the pay was set. Work was usually paid based on a monthly agreement in both private and state employ, but in a private business one could ask for hourly pay. When he asked me how much I wanted to be paid, I told him 80 dinars per hour, which was in the upper bracket. Without any hesitation, he agreed, which was wonderful since my mother and sisters needed financial help.

I had yet to tell him, though, that I was unable to work on Saturdays. When I told him, he was perplexed and remained silent for a long time.

Then he said, "No, no, that will be very difficult since Saturday is the busiest work day."

I told him I would work long hours during the week and make up my time, and after further thought, he said he would keep me. That suited me very well.

My plan was to work only about a month and then attempt to leave the country.

The Vacant Seat

It is interesting to note, however, that conditions or circumstances can play an important part in making decisions. The job was very good, the pay was good, and the whole atmosphere was good at work. The city where I worked was very nice. The climate in this coastal town was very enjoyable; one could swim all year around in the Adriatic Sea. The beaches were wonderful to walk on or simply to recline in the sun and relax.

After a month at work I felt I should start examining the border. There was a soccer field near the border, so I decided I would go "watch" a number of soccer games, when in reality I was more interested in looking at the border and figuring out the best way to approach and cross it rather than the soccer team. As the time went by though, I somehow lost the urgent need to leave, and I started to enjoy the security of my job.

My employer was a war invalid, and as the Bible says, some of God's people in the past found grace with those for whom they worked.

I, too, seemed to have found grace with this man. He kept suggesting to me that when I returned from army service he would let me have the business with the provision that I pay him a certain percentage. These kinds of arrangements were legal and common. He told me a number of times he wanted me to take over the business, and he even enrolled me in a designer school where we both went to improve our skills in fashion design and to learn new techniques in the clothing industry. All this was in order to keep me with him in business.

He also assigned me an apprentice, Eddy, who I had to teach. She was a lovely young girl, about seventeen years of age, while I was twenty. She was very intelligent and learned quickly. Her parents were both communist party members, and when I told her that my uncles and ny brother George were also members of the party, her parents wanted to meet me.

I had to cook for myself, and since I worked long hours, I had very little time to prepare meals. I was rather thin, and when this young lady realized my situation, she suggested I eat at her place, saying her mother would cook for me.

When I told her I was vegetarian, she told me she would ask her mother to prepare vegetarian food for me. To my surprise, her mother agreed, and after agreeing on a price for her to cook the evening meals for me, I started eating with them.

Everything was going so well I decided to stay in Yugoslavia longer than I'd first planned. I also knew my mother needed financial support. She still had my two younger sisters with her, and she had very little in the way of support. I was sending her enough money for food and clothes every month. This was another reason for not leaving the country yet. I felt that if I was to go, according my original plan, she would be left in a difficult situation. My older brothers were not in a position to help as they had families and they needed all the money they earned.

So I kept delaying or postponing my plan to leave.

Chapter 13

Taking Two Weeks Vacation

After working for ten months, I decided to take some of holidays I was entitled to. My employer was happy to let me have this holiday. He was still saying that as soon as I finished my military service he would hand the business over to me.

During the time I worked there, I met a lot of people, but I was overly cautious in disclosing to anyone my eventual plan to leave the country. Interestingly, I met a fine family who attended the Church of the Nazarene, the same religion my mother had been part of for eleven years. As I did not work on Saturdays, I would often spend my time in parks or walking along the beach where I could have privacy for reading and prayers.

One particular Saturday afternoon as I was walking along the street toward my apartment, I heard a lovely Christian melody being played. I stopped to listen, wondering where it was coming from. I realized it was coming from the upper floor. As I went up the first flight of stairs, there was a corridor with doors to apartments. I walked to each door and listened to see if I could find out where the music was coming from. My heart was beating fast, and I prayed the music would not stop until I found it. Then finally, as I put my ear to one particular door, I could hear the music coming from inside. I stood there in front of the door for a while, thoroughly enjoying the glorious melody before working up enough courage to knock.

As I knocked I heard footsteps approach. I felt somewhat apprehensive, but I quickly decided what I would say as to the reason for my intrusion. As the door opened there stood a very kind looking person, a real motherly type. She even looked similar to my own mother, just larger in stature. She asked me what I wanted, and I told her about the wonderful music I had heard while walking on the street, and she said, "This is the music that touches my heart."

She then welcomed me in and introduced me to her son who was playing an organ. Our friendship was instant. Through their friendship, I met many more people, including a family who were members of the Seventh-day Adventist Church. Meeting this family was good for me as it gave me the opportunity to have company on Sabbath. We met in their house and enjoyed good fellowship together.

Through them I met another lady who owned a swimwear shop. She also had two teenage sons. Her husband was not a very caring man, and she had to manage the shop as well as care for the children. She

The Vacant Seat

was a wonderful person, and she too came to the meetings on Saturday afternoons. It was left to me to conduct all the meetings.

We often talked about our social situation as a result of the Sabbath and the general situation of Christians. Although the government gave certain freedoms, if one had to complete military service, the government gave no provision for conscientious objectors or noncombatants. And keeping the Sabbath was completely unthinkable. Everyone had to go to the army; it was not voluntary, and the law was harsh. When you reached twenty years of age, you were conscripted. The only people exempt were those who were ill and deemed not fit to serve.

When I turned twenty, I was called for the military health check, and after two weeks I was notified I was fit to serve in the army. They also wrote to me that I would receive a call to report to an army department in due time. I could be called at any time.

By the time I was twenty-one, the call had still not arrived. This was good for me. It gave me time to work and prepare myself to leave the country.

Why did I want to avoid serving in the army? It wasn't because I was disloyal to my country, which I loved, but I knew that if I entered the army and refused to carry a gun, I would be court-martialed and sentenced to three or four years in prison with hard labor. Even in prison they would force me to work on Saturdays, and if I refused there would be beatings, torture, solitary confinement for weeks, and deprivation of food. Basic essentials would be just enough to keep me alive. Some of the young men conscripted to the army who were members of my faith barely survived years of torture, and their health was damaged for life.

To me, even though I loved my country, especially the province where I was born with its beautiful fertile fields, vineyards, and orchards, I felt that for the sake of freedom I had to leave. The most difficult thought was that of leaving my mother, brothers, and sisters. But I had to leave, for I knew freedom was the most precious thing in life.

I purchased a train ticket for my vacation. I planned to travel to my village early in August 1959. I was to travel to Belgrade by international train from Rome, Italy, and when in Belgrade, I had to change to a local train that would take me to Beska, the nearest town to my village. Finally the day came to leave, and I packed my bags and said goodbye to the people I worked with and my employer. I told him I would be gone for two weeks. The trip was good, and upon my arrival, it was wonderful to see my family after almost a year of absence. It was Thursday evening when I arrived at my brother's house where my mother and my sisters lived. After a long talk about my life so far from home, we all finally went to sleep.

I got up early the next morning, a Friday, and went to my mother's garden. She grew the most wonderful vegetables, fruits, and herbs, and it felt so wonderful to be at home. While walking through the garden, I felt like staying there and not going back to my work and also not leaving Yugoslavia. The

Taking Two Weeks Vacation

beautiful fields, the lovely smell of the garden, the flowers my dear mother grew—all felt like paradise. I thought about how wonderful it would be to stay and never leave.

After an hour I returned to the house, and my younger sister Mira told me, rather agitated, "Brother, you must go immediately to the council chambers. Two men in uniform came asking for you; they looked like police. I looked, but I could not find you. I told them you are here somewhere, most likely you had gone for a walk. They told me that as soon as you returned you must go and see why they are looking for you."

That message spoiled my serenity, my wonderful peaceful thoughts, and I was greatly disturbed. What do the police want now? I wondered.

I had been caught twice trying to escape the country, but I had been sent to prison both times, so what did they want? This puzzled me very much. After hearing what Mira said, my older brother Predrag, who was at home, told me, "Brother, do not worry. I know all the people there. I will go find out why they are looking for you."

He left soon after breakfast. It did not take long, and he soon returned waving a piece of paper. "Brother," he said, "you are to be a soldier in thirteen days time!"

I could not believe what I was hearing. I was in shock. Almost ten months ago I had left my home with the intention of leaving the country because of the military service, yet because of my good life I had delayed my plan, and now I was trapped. I was at the other end of the country, the far eastern border. To go back to the Italian border seemed impossible.

All the details were written on the paper—the day I must report to the army unit, the place to go, and the many rules prior to actually being in the armed forces and becoming a soldier.

One of the rules was the one hundred kilometer radius. If caught outside that zone, I would be arrested and tried by the military court as a deserter. The punishment for such an act was severe with at least nine years hard labor in prison. There was no time to lose. I had to make a quick decision, and I did. I decided to travel back to the city where I worked, which was more than 1,500 kilometers away. Whether I would make it all the way there, or if I would be caught, there was no time to think. It was Friday, so I stayed indoors all day to avoid neighbors and other people from seeing me. The next day was Sabbath, and again I stayed indoors. The meetings were held in our home since there was no church building.

When all the members of the church, in whom I knew I could trust, I told them of my intention and asked for their prayers. They were glad to see me after such a long time, but they were sad I was leaving and also worried about what might happen to me. We spent all day in worship and prayer. My mother prayed earnestly with tears running down her noble face. When the day was over, after dinner, which I could not eat, I packed my bags and some food and started walking out of the house.

Everyone followed me. Instead of going along the road, I went through the fields in order to avoid anyone seeing me. It was dark, the sun had set, and after walking for a while, I told them all to go back.

The Vacant Seat

But most ignored my request and kept walking with me. Finally one after another said goodbye and returned to their homes. The last one to return was my mother. She kept walking with me, holding me tight. Through her tears, she asked, "My dear son, where are you going?"

Her question seemed to pierce my heart, and I told her, "My dear mother, I do not know, but if the Lord of heaven hears your prayer, my prayer, and the prayers of all those that prayed for me, then I should arrive at my intended destination safely. But if not, then I have no answer."

I then told her to go back to the house as it was late and not safe to walk through the fields by herself at night. It was not safe to walk through the fields even in the daytime, for there were crimes of rape, robbery, and even murder. Finally my dear precious mother embraced me and, although crying uncontrollably, offered a heartfelt prayer. She held me in her arms and, with the little strength she had left in her, said goodbye to me. As she turned to walk back, I watched her, my heart aching more for her than for myself.

After about an hour I arrived at the railway station and boarded a train to Belgrade. After arriving in Belgrade, I went to the church as I had more than two hours until I boarded the train to Koper. It was the same express train that went to Rome, and while I wished I could have gone all the way to Rome, it was not possible. Instead, I would get off the train at the last railway station in Yugoslavia before the train crossed into Italy.

At the church I met three elderly people who, after telling them of my intention, prayed for me. After a time of prayer I said goodbye to them and walked back to the station. As I arrived and boarded the train, I felt a terrible weight in my chest. I found it hard to breath. The thought of being caught terrified me. But there was another problem. I had told my employer I would be back in two weeks time, and now I was coming back three days later.

What would I tell him? The thought troubled me. I felt anxious and troubled at the same time. If only I could stop thinking, if only I could sleep through this nightmare and wake up in Italy. But I had to face my situation and somehow gather strength, calm down, and keep going. I prayed earnestly for wisdom and safety.

Finding my compartment and seat number, I placed by bags on the shelf above the seat and sat by the window waiting for the train to start. I greeted the people opposite me but did not converse with them further. The seat next to me was still vacant, and I was anxious as to who would be seated next to me since I knew all the seats were reserved.

Provided I arrived safely, I decided I would tell my employer the truth about the military call. I would tell him I came to say goodbye to him. I was sure he would be happy to hear this because the sooner I finished military service the sooner he could give me the business. I had no intention of telling him the rest of my plan, which was to escape on foot.

Taking Two Weeks Vacation

My mind still wondered, Who will sit next to me? I was completely preoccupied with these thoughts. For some reason I felt that whoever occupied the seat was to have some sort of profound impact on me.

The time it took for the train to start going seemed like an eternity. I looked at my watch every few minutes. The departure time had already passed, and the train was still standing still. Then, just before it started, a new passenger came into our compartment.

When I saw him I was frozen, finding it difficult to breath. My senses became numb. The passenger was a big police officer in full uniform, and of course, his seat was the one still vacant next to me. Before he sat down he put his bags on the overhead shelf. Then he greeted me and made himself comfortable without removing his uniform coat. I too was dressed in my suit with my coat on. (It was the custom that one dressed when traveling as if going to some formal function.)

I felt totally at a loss as to why it had to be a police officer who would sit next to me. Soon after he sat down he started a conversation about the summer and the lovely weather we were having. It was August 20, 1959, and it was indeed wonderful warm weather, a true southern European summer.

After a short conversation, we just sat enjoying the smooth sound of the train moving forward. In the silence my mind raced faster than the train. I couldn't stop thinking about the dire consequences should he discover that in another few kilometers I was about to become a fugitive, a deserter from the army.

At times I felt as if I was going to break out in a cold sweat, but I had to be in control of my feelings, every movement, the tone of my voice, and my whole deportment. I feared that should he notice my nervousness, he would become suspicious and start watching my every move. In addition, when we were 100 kilometers from Belgrade, he would have the right to arrest me and take me off the train at the next stop.

After traveling for some time, we arrived at the first city in Croatia. The 100-kilometer zone had already passed, and now, according to the law, I was officially a military deserter. Should I be caught now, imprisonment would quickly follow.

After a while my companion, the police officer, started another conversation. He asked me about my qualifications, my profession, relatives, and so on. I told him many things about me, but I was very selective. As our conversation was in full swing, the first inspection came. Before coming to our compartment, I heard the man asking for travel documents and also asking for identity cards. When he finally came to our compartment, he inspected the travel documents of the passengers opposite us.

I put my hand in my coat pocket to take out my ticket and my identity card; however, as he turned to us, he just gave us a quick glance and turned to the door and walked out. I was surprised. I felt that he would not check the police officer, for no one checked or questioned the police, but me? I thought it was rather unusual that he did not even ask me for my travel documents. What was more unusual was that he did it on an international train—a train that was going to Rome.

The Vacant Seat

By now it was past midnight, and although I was very tired, I could not sleep. After a while, the police officer, who had been asleep, woke up, and we continued our conversation. We were long past 100 kilometers and were going through Croatia when another inspection occurred. I was sure that this time I would be asked for my travel documents and perhaps even asked where I was going and why.

I heard the inspector asking other passengers many questions, even asking if they had their passports, and my worries began to increase. As the inspector arrived at our compartment, after checking the passengers opposite us, the same inspector repeated the same act. He just looked at the police officer and me and left the compartment. A new thought came to me, something that seemed too good to be true. Perhaps this man thought that I, too, was a police officer in civilian clothing, which would have made me much higher ranking than the one in uniform. Perhaps this was why he was not asking for my documents. He would not even dare to question a detective.

The train continued on its journey. By now we were hundreds of kilometers from Belgrade, and I felt as if I was a true fugitive. Should I be caught, I could not think of an explanation for traveling. As we entered the state of Slovenia, new inspectors came around asking for travel documents. In addition, they asked many other questions such as where people were going and why, what was their occupation, and who did they know in the place they were going. This time, I prayed to the Lord of heaven and asked Him to be by my side and give me the words to speak should I be asked any questions. As I heard them coming to our compartment, I felt as if this was my last few minutes of freedom.

But two inspectors entered our compartment, checked the passengers opposite us, and then, after giving us a quick glance, left. I began to wonder if my earlier thoughts were correct, that they regarded both of us as people not to be questioned. For my companion, his uniform made it obvious who he was. However, for me, something or someone must be prevented them from speaking to me. The thought came to me, Could the Lord have sent His angel in the form of a police officer to protect me? Could it be true?

I was still too unsure to entertain such a notions, and by now night was coming to an end, and dawn was approaching. I could see light, and the passengers were growing restless. As the train was approaching Ljubljana, the capital of Slovenia, more inspections were held and more questions asked. But at each inspection we were simply looked at and left alone.

There were two more stations before the train came to the Italian border. At that point all the passengers would be required to disembark and walk through the inspection gate to be thoroughly checked before entering Italy. The train would cross the border without any passengers on board. After it was inspected, it would return, and all those going to Italy would re-board the train and continue their journey. Announcements were repeated that all passengers who were not going to Italy had to disembark at the next two stations. As we came to the next station, my companion took his bags and said goodbye to me. I had mixed feelings as I said goodbye to him. By now I was sure he had been sent by God to be my protector.

Taking Two Weeks Vacation

This man never once asked me as to where I was going or the reason for my trip. It was not much farther, and I too had to get off the train. As I left the train and boarded the bus to travel to the city where I worked, I faced the new concern of telling my employer the truth about the military call and my return to say goodbye to him and his family. It worked well, and although he was surprised to see me, after explaining my actions, he was very happy and again repeated that his business would be mine as soon as I returned from the army. I hadn't said I was going to the army, just that I had been called up and had come to say goodbye.

There were nine days left before I had to report to my designated army unit. I didn't have much time left, so I had to act quickly. I had to inform my friend, with whom I had made an agreement to escape to Italy that we had to leave.

My employer decided to send me off by taking me to hear the world famous Italian singer Mario Lanza, who was visiting our small but well-known city for a concert. I decided that this was the night I must go as most of the police would be occupied with Mario Lanza and his entourage. There would be many people coming from the surrounding districts, and the streets would be buzzing with masses of visitors.

My employer gave me money to buy four tickets for the performance for him, his wife, Eddy, and me. As soon as I received the money, I went to Eddy and told her the good news. Eddy was beside herself with excitement. She grabbed me and started dancing around the room. For her and many others this was a once-in-a-lifetime opportunity.

I gave her the money and told her I was going to get ready. As I was leaving, she called out, "Don't be too long! We cannot be late. I want to be early for a show of this magnitude."

I said nothing, simply because I could not. My heart was beating so fast I felt as if it was going to jump out of my chest.

There was no time to delay. I had to go to the border. I went to my room, tore up all papers and letters I had received since I arrived, chose my best clothes and packed them in my suitcase, and slowly walked downstairs, making sure I was not heard or seen by my employer's wife or children.

Chapter 14

The Escape

It was August 24, 1959.

After successfully leaving my employer's home without being noticed, I went to my friend's house. When I arrived and told him this was the night to make our dash for freedom, he hesitated, telling me that he was not ready to go. Not yet.

I told him I had to go, that I had only nine days left before I had to report to the military. "If you cannot go now then I must go by myself," I told him.

He then said, "In that case we go."

To my surprise, he took two bags. In one he had his clothes, but the other was empty. I asked what the second bag was for, and he said it was in case of an emergency. Without any further questions, we left.

By now it was dark, and the Mario Lanza performance would be starting soon. Poor Eddy must have been frantic wondering what had happened to me, but I tried to dismiss those thoughts. As we walked past one of the hotels, my friend said he was hungry and we should go to the hotel to eat. I told him there was not a moment to lose. But he insisted, and we went in. He ordered some food and asked if I wanted something. I told him no. Even if I was hungry, I could not eat. Every moment was precious, and I prayed to stay as calm as possible.

After eating, as the waiter came to bring the bill, my friend looked at me and asked a very strange question, "Comrade, didn't our comrades order some cigarettes?"

Without waiting for my answer, he turned to the waiter and ordered enough cigarettes to fill one of his suitcases. I told him in no uncertain terms I did not want him to carry cigarettes, since it was my third attempt to leave the country, and if we were caught carrying so many cigarettes, we would be in an even more dangerous situation.

His reply was calm, "You have nothing to do with what is in this case since I will be carrying it."

I said nothing further. After paying the waiter for the meal and the cigarettes, we left the hotel and headed for the bus that would take us twelve kilometers from the city of Koper. By now Eddy and my employer must have been very concerned about my whereabouts, as it was time for the concert to start. I tried to dismiss these thoughts and concentrate on our journey, but the more I tried the more persistent my thoughts were.

Finally the bus stopped at a small village, and we got off the bus with a few other passengers. It was dark by now, and to our good fortune, there was a forest across the road. As soon as the other passengers disappeared, we made our dash for the forest. Once there I felt somewhat safer. It was dark, and we were not sure of the exact direction we had to go, but we had a good idea where the border was.

Both loaded with heavy suitcases, we walked. The walk through the forest was hampered by the undergrowth and rocks, and we had to climb many steep mountains, some of which were at times almost vertical and rugged. It was also a moonless night, which made our journey even slower and more difficult.

Despite the roughness of the terrain, we passed by houses where mountain people lived. "Mountain people" would dig into the hill, build a house, and then construct a high retaining wall to make a garden. They planted vegetables and vineyards along these steep slopes.

We walked for a few hours, stopping at times for short rests. But we were always aware of our precarious situation, so we kept pushing forward to reach the border. At times, because of the darkness of the night, we were often unsure where we were. We saw a few dwellings with the lights on inside, which we kept well away from.

But despite trying to avoid those houses, at one point we found ourselves in one of the gardens with the high retaining walls. To add to our troubles, the owners had dogs that started barking. We ran as fast as we could to get away from the dogs and also, possibly, the owners of that house. As we ran we came to the end of the garden and had to jump down from the wall. Unable to see how far we had to jump, we threw our bags down. My friend jumped far, but I jumped straight down, not seeing the big tree below me. I landed between the wall and the tree, hitting my face on the tree with terrific force.

As the impact hit me, I fell to the ground semi-unconscious. I tried to get to my feet, but I felt dizzy, and then I felt a sharp pain and heavy bleeding from my nose. It was a terrible blow indeed. Despite this, I still tried to get up and walk. Not realizing how hurt I was, my companion urged me to keep going, but after a few minutes I could not walk at all. I had to rest.

After a while we made another attempt to continue our journey, but it was with great difficulty. Finally, I decided to leave my bag behind and try to walk without it. I took my Bible out and a shirt to try to stop the bleeding. But despite all the efforts, after a short time I could not go any further.

I urged my friend to go on so he would not be caught, but since I could no longer walk, I resigned to my destiny. But my friend refused to leave me. He continued to urge me to keep going, no matter how slow the journey. But it was to no avail. I simply had to stop, which meant that come daylight I would likely be found. I didn't even want to imagine what the consequences would be for my actions.

I told my companion to go on and save himself, but he told me something I have never forgotten. "We have started this journey together, and we will end it together, whether in Italy or in prison in Yugoslavia."

The Vacant Seat

I could not believe what I was hearing. Here was a man who I hardly knew, more of an acquaintance than a friend. This man, who did not profess to be a Christian, was virtually giving his life for me. It was far beyond my weary mind and my almost broken body. He suggested we lay down on the ground and rest. I agreed and within a few minutes I was fast asleep.

When I woke I felt better, and at the same time, I was in a state of shock. The left side of my face felt numb, swollen, and very painful to touch. I could not touch my nose, which I figured was broken. It was filled with dry blood, and I could not breathe through it.

The sun was already high, and only then did it occur to me that we were still in Yugoslavia. I was thankful no one had found us, and at the same time, panic gripped me knowing that we could be discovered at any time. I looked for my friend and saw him sleeping a short distance away.

It was August 25, 1959.

I got up and thanked God for helping me to feel somewhat better. I went over to my friend and woke him up. I then asked him if he was aware we were still in Yugoslavia. Very calmly he answered, "Yes, I am aware, but do not panic."

Next, we climbed a very steep hill to the top. For me, it was the climb of my life. Every moment I felt as if I was going to faint, but I kept going. An unseen force seemed to be pushing me upward, and despite enormous weakness and loss of blood, I kept going. My companion did not have it easy either, with his two full suitcases, but he kept ahead of me and kept urging me to keep the pace with him. Finally, after an almost supernatural effort, we reached the summit. The view was breathtaking.

There in front of us lay the sprawling city of Trieste. We were beyond ourselves, feeling as if we were already there. We were so near and yet so far.

We were still in Yugoslavia, and the greatest hurdle was yet to come, crossing the border without being caught. Many foreboding thoughts went through my mind. What if we are caught by a guard dog as I was caught on my first attempt? What if the soldiers surprise us from the bushes? What if they see us and shoot at us without warning?

The what ifs kept invading my mind. Because it was his first attempt, my friend didn't have these same thought. I must admit, although I was praying, somehow my faith seemed to have left me at the very time I needed it.

As we started our descent down the hill, we could clearly see the border. At this stage we did not see any soldiers. We saw the path and the low wire with signs saying the approach of any unauthorized persons was strictly forbidden. In order to not make even the slightest noise, we took our shoes off and, instead of walking, we crouched stealthily as a wild beast does when it sneaks up on its prey. As we came closer to the border, we saw one soldier walking with his machine gun strapped on his right shoulder.

We immediately stopped. In total silence we carefully observed his movements to see if he may have heard us. But after a few moments we realized he did not hear us, and so we kept walking. Another concern was that he may have a dog that would quickly be alerted to our scent even though we had hot capsicum powder that we sprinkled as we walked, hoping that this would distract any dogs. It was not long before we saw another soldier walking from the opposite direction toward the soldier we had already seen. As they came together they stopped for a few moments to talk and light up a cigarette. We waited in total silence, crouched to the ground.

Although it was a short conversation, to us it seemed like an eternity. We were anxious, not knowing what move they were going to make with us barely 100 meters from them. Fortunately, nature was kind to us. Just inside the border was very thick tall grass where we were able to hide and observe our surroundings.

After what seemed like forever, the two soldiers saluted and moved on. We waited until they were a long distance from each other, and making sure there were no other soldiers, we made our move toward the border.

There was not a moment to waste. We literally had to run for our lives. No one was in the sight. As we approached we saw the border had wire running about forty centimeters high. We had to jump over carefully so as to not trip the wire, which would raise an alarm or even warning flares, something I had learned about in prison after the second time I was caught.

As we jumped over the wire, we ran until we crossed over into no man's land near the Italian border. We didn't know if the soldiers had spotted us while we were still in no man's land or whether they would be in pursuit or even if they would try to stop us by shooting at us. Taking no chances, we simply ran as fast as we could.

We were expecting to be stopped by the Italian border soldiers, but to our surprise, there were none in sight. The only thing we saw were signs stating that this was the Italian border with Italian flags printed on the ground. Signs in Italian and Serbian/Croatian stated that unauthorized personnel were strictly forbidden in this area. This only made us run faster. Weak as I was, some power seemed to take hold of me, and I felt as if I was virtually carried. I felt no tiredness, no dizziness, and no shortness of breath, all of the feelings I had experienced just a few hours earlier.

Without saying a word to each other, we ran as does prey from its deadly pursuer. We were running for our lives. Never even glancing back, we kept going through the thick grass, feeling as if God had planted it specifically to hide us from any predators, whether animal or human.

After running for about an hour, I started feeling very tired and extremely light headed. Without saying a word to my companion, I fell to the ground exhausted. Seeing me on the ground, he did likewise. Then summoning all the strength that was left in me, I stood up and asked him to kneel with me in prayer.

The Vacant Seat

Not being a praying person, he was surprised at my request. "Why pray now; we have made it?"

I replied, "This is the very reason we should pray now. To thank our heavenly Father, to thank our God and Savior Jesus Christ for bringing us safely to this place."

Being polite and respectful of my faith, he said, "If you feel like praying, then go ahead and pray."

To me, this was the prayer of my life. I cannot recall the exact words I uttered, but I do remember repeating again and again "Thank you, Lord; thank you, Lord."

After I had finished praying, we continued on our journey toward the city of Trieste.

For a while, we kept silent. But then he spoke. "You religious people seem to be fearful and at the same time have some mysterious strength that keeps you going regardless of your physical or mental condition."

He then went on to tell me that if I could see how I looked in a mirror I would probably faint. He told me the complete left side of my face was one big dry blood bruise. I was not surprised at this because both my nose and the whole side of my face pounded and was excruciating to touch.

Our clothes were filthy with mud and grass stains. As we came upon a road, there was water along the road, and he suggested I try to wash a little, saying that if children saw me they would run to their mother screaming that they had seen a monster.

I told him that it would not be the first time children were afraid of seeing me nor adults, and I went on to tell him about when I was born and how my uncle had proclaimed that I was ugly.

My companion laughed, "You are not that ugly, but the bruised face does not help."

With his careful help, I washed my face as much as the pain would allow, leaving the congealed blood so the heavy bleeding would not continue.

As we walked along the road toward the city of Trieste, which was still a fair distance away, to our joy we noticed a bus approaching. Not having any Italian currency, we wondered how we could pay for our fares should the bus stop at our signal. To our surprise, the bus driver stopped and offered us a lift. Not speaking Italian we simply said, "Trieste." He nodded and indicated to us to sit on the vacant seats just behind him.

The journey to the city of Trieste took about an hour, and as we didn't have currency, my friend offered the bus driver two packets of cigarettes as payment. To my surprise, the driver took the cigarettes, and we were dropped off at the city center. Upon getting off the bus, my companion told me, "Now if I did not have cigarettes, you would have had to walk all the way to the city."

"I am still opposing to cigarettes and smoking," I said.

As we walked along the streets, we saw a bank. Its name drew my attention because in Yugoslavia I had never seen a bank by such a name. It was the "Bank of Santus Spiritus," meaning the Bank of the Holy Spirit. Since we needed Italian currency, we went in and exchanged some money.

We felt ready to face the future now that we had money to buy food and necessities.

Chapter 15

Goodbye, My Friend

As we walked out of the bank, my companion, who had the same name as me, extended his hand and said, "Goodbye, my friend."

I was momentarily stunned.

Not knowing what to think, I asked him, "What do you mean by saying goodbye?"

Then he told me his plan.

He told me the Italian government had an agreement with the Yugoslavian government to send most of the refugees back to Yugoslavia, and since he did not want that to happen to him, he had decided to go to France.

He told me there should be no problem to cross the border into France from Italy. If he managed to reach Paris, the French authorities would not send him back, but if he was apprehended before he reached Paris, they could return him to Italy and not Yugoslavia, since he had come from Italy.

I asked him who gave him that information because it could be wrong. But he told me that his mind was made up. Before we parted he offered for me to come with him, but I told him, "I'll take the chance and apply to the Italian authorities for protection."

Very reluctantly, we said goodbye to each other.

As I watched him walk away, a strange feeling came upon me. I could not comprehend who this man was who said goodbye to me. The man who, a few hours ago while still in the forest and still in Yugoslavia, had risked his freedom and possibly his life for me. As I watched my friend walk away, I felt strangely alone. For the first time I realized I was in a strange country, and although I could read the advertising signs, I did not understand what they were telling me. And the people talked, shouted, and greeted each other, yet I did not understand anything.

How would I communicate? Where would I buy food? I was hungry, and I felt weary from last night's ordeal. Many perplexing questions came to my mind.

Despite my perplexity, I felt I needed a plan. I needed to find a shop like a news agency where I could buy postcards to send to my loved ones in Yugoslavia letting them know I had made it to Italy. Fortunately, it did not take long to find just the shop I needed. It was well stocked with very beautiful

The Vacant Seat

postcards, so I chose about twenty nice cards. Then I wrote to my mother, my brothers and sisters, my relatives, my friends, and a number of people from church. I did not write long letters; I simply wrote, "I made it." I gave no address since I did not have one.

The next move was to visit a couple I had met in Yugoslavia at one of our church meetings. They were Italians but spoke Serbo-Croatian. During their visit to Yugoslavia at one of the meetings, they gave me their address. They told me if I ever managed to get to Trieste to pay them a visit. Now that I was in Trieste, I decided to take that opportunity.

I was in the center of the city with many buses going in all directions. It was a very nice day with the summer sun still shining. I went to the bus stop, and after asking a number of drivers, I finally found the right bus. I showed the address to the driver who pointed for me to sit just behind him. I could tell from his body language he would tell me where I needed to get off the bus.

After traveling for about forty-five minutes, the driver told me to get off and pointed to the street sign. Sure enough, it was the street where my church brethren lived. As I got off the bus, I thanked the driver. As I walked along the street, I looked for the number of the house. I soon realized it was a block of apartments. Their apartment was on the second floor. I rang the bell, but there was no answer. As I continued ringing, the lady next door heard my prolonged ringing, came out, and started talking to me in Italian.

I just shrugged my shoulders, and pointing to myself, I said, "No Italian."

She then, to my great surprise, started talking to me in Yugoslav. She told me they were out selling books and would be home toward the evening. For me it was rather disappointing, and not knowing what to do, I thanked the lady and walked back to the street.

As I walked along the street, a police officer came up to me and started talking to me in Italian. Again I told him, "No Italian." He then spoke to me in Yugoslav. He asked me where I had come from, and after telling him that I came from Yugoslavia, he asked to see my passport. I told him I did not have passport.

He then asked how I had come to Italy.

I told him I had escaped from Yugoslavia on foot and that it took me all night. He then asked me what my plans were, where did I intend to go?

I told him I planned to report to the Italian authorities. He then told me to follow him, and he called another police officer who arrived within minutes in a police van. It was strange and somewhat fearful to be in the police van again, particularly because I did not know where they were taking me. There was an awful possibility they would take me straight back over the border to Yugoslavia; I'd heard similar stories during my second imprisonment.

After traveling for about thirty minutes, the van stopped. When the back door opened, I saw one police officer and two Catholic nuns standing by the door. The police officer told me to come out, and the nuns smiled at me. Confused, I did not know what to think, but I admit the friendly nuns gave me hope that I would not be returned, not just yet.

They took me inside what looked to be a large house rather than a convent. Once inside the nuns brought me clothes—trousers, shirts, underwear, shoes, and socks. Then they showed me the bathroom. It was wonderful to have a warm shower and be able to refresh my weary body.

After I was dressed, the nuns took me to the dining room and offered me lunch. On the plate was meat and salad, so I told them I was a vegetarian. They gave me a look of surprise. I was very thin, and I wondered if they were thinking, "It is no wonder he is so thin; he does not eat good food."

Then they had a short conversation among themselves. Although I did not understand what they were saying, I thought they must be wondering what to give me to eat. Then I heard them repeat the word "fish." It was the first time I had heard that word. Soon after that they brought me fish, telling me something that I assumed was "Is this okay?"

But to their dismay even this was not good for me. I just said no, and I pointed to macaroni and salad. I said, "Dobro, dobro," which means good, good. They burst into laughter. Then one of the nuns went and brought me another very large plate of macaroni. They just shook their heads. Being very hungry, I ate a lot—I have perhaps never eaten so much macaroni in my life.

There were some other people, perhaps refugees like me, but since I could not speak their language, we could not communicate. After staying there two days, the police came and took me to the large refugee camp, I was overwhelmed by the size of it and the people that were there. It seemed to me the whole world was there. There were people from all over the world, all colors and races. I was shown the room where I would be staying; there were about twenty-five beds in the room. I was happy my bed was in the corner right next to the wall. Then they brought me some more clothes and took me to the different places around the camp.

After writing down a few things about me, I was informed I would be questioned by the authorities. After a few days they called me to the office. After reporting to the front desk, the young lady pointed toward the room I needed to go in, and after entering the man behind the desk almost immediately started shouting at me. He was worse than any interrogator who had questioned me in Yugoslavia.

He didn't ask me questions, but rather he made statements about me. He accused me of being an adventurer, running away from my responsibilities and expecting to go to a western country in order to lie on my back and have food dropped into my mouth by fair maidens. I didn't have a chance to say a word. I just kept quiet and waited for my chance to tell him my reasons for being here. After a while he gave me that chance. I told him the reason I left Yugoslavia was because of my beliefs. I told him I was called to do military service and because of my beliefs I had to refuse, resulting in me being imprisoned for a number of years. I lived in a communist country where there was no freedom of choice. One had to do what they told you, and if you refused, you were thrown in prison for many years.

The Vacant Seat

My interrogator, who spoke Yugoslavian, appeared to ignore what I was saying. He continued shouting at the top of his voice. He threatened me that I would be sent back to Yugoslavia, but despite his attitude, I kept repeating my reasons for leaving Yugoslavia. The secretary recorded our conversation. After about two to three hours, he told me to go. I left in shock, hoping and praying his threats would not come true.

Life in the camp was difficult. Food was a big problem since I was a vegetarian. I ate mainly spaghetti and salads as there was no fresh fruits or vegetables.

After three weeks I was called to the office again. This time about twenty-five of us were interviewed and questioned by the international police. We all had to wait in the corridor, and one by one they called us in for questioning. We were anxious and worried because they would decide if we stayed or if we would have to return to our countries. None of us wanted this to happen, and as people went in, we could hear shouting and threatening.

Then came my turn.

There were about ten people seated at the very long desk, and the one questioning me spoke in Yugoslavian.

"How long have you been a communist party member?" he asked me.

I told him I had never been a communist party member because I was a Christian and communists did not want Christians in their membership.

He asked if any of my family members were communists. My answer was truthful. I told him that my oldest brother was a communist party member.

He then asked me the reason I left the country. I repeated the answer I had given to the Italian interrogator. I stated that because of military service I had no freedom of choice. Should I refuse to do combat service I would be in prison for the minimum of three years, this is why I wanted to go to a free country.

They asked me which country I intended to go to, and I told them I intended to immigrate to the United States.

Then he asked me another question, "Being a young man, when you become a citizen of the United States, they might call you to serve in the military there. Since you did not want to serve in a communist country, would you serve the military in the United States?"

"No, I believe in peace not war. Nations should be able to live peacefully amongst themselves."

He then asked me one more question. "What is the name of the church you are a member of?"

I gave him the name, and he told me I could go.

After I came out the people who were with me were surprised they had not heard any shouting or threatening. They asked me questions, and I answered accordingly. After this we returned to the camp and started our anxious wait for the results.

We all knew the decision would be crucial. I personally hoped, trusted, and prayed I would not be sent back. Some of us tried to get information from the office in the camp. We asked if we had been granted permission to stay in Italy and then to immigrate to another country, but no answer was given to us. We were only told the answer would be released in due time.

One month after I arrived at the camp in Trieste I was called to the office. I was told I had been granted the right to stay in Italy, and the next day I would be moved to another camp. The camp I was to be sent to was in the city of Latina, sixty kilometers south of Rome. They gave me no written documentation stating I could stay, so naturally I was anxious as to whether they were telling me the truth. The reason for this anxiety was because they were telling everyone they were being transported to another camp, when in reality the majority were being taken back to Yugoslavia.

I prayed more than ever that I would not be taken back. I experienced many sleepless night. Before our scheduled departure, I called a member of our church in the city of Trieste and requested that he go to the main railway station and wait for me at the platform for the train scheduled to go to Rome. The man I'd called was Brother Tinta, his grandson Giordano is a church member in Italy.

At the camp in Trieste, all the exit gates were closed, and nobody got a permit to go out of the camp. This was a normal procedure, and during that month this procedure did not worry me. But now the situation was different. When they called me to the office and told me they were transporting me to another camp in the south of Italy, I tried to seek some assurance that I was being sent to another camp. The answer I received was simply confirmed, and no further details were given.

Many who were told they are being transported to another camp did not believe the officials and tried to escape from the camp by scaling the walls and jumping out. Those whose rooms had windows facing open fields often jumped from the windows in order to avoid being sent back to Yugoslavia.

As it happened the room where I was staying had windows overlooking the fields. Very often during my stay I would look through the window at the fertile fields with vegetables and other green crops that reminded me very much of my home back in my village, back home where my dear mother tenderly cared for her garden.

At times I even wished I was back at home walking through my mother's garden, but that was all in the past. It was not possible to go back; I had a new direction in my life, and I had to pursue it.

As the days progressed, my friends at the camp urged me to jump through the window and try to escape from being returned to Yugoslavia. For a while I entertained this thought, but I decided not to do it. Instead I prayed.

Finally we were called to the office to receive our travel documents. After we received our papers, we were told to go to our rooms, pack our belongings, and go to the front office where we would board police vans that would take us to the railway station. We were a group of twenty-five, a relatively small group, and it was known that smaller groups were normally taken back to Yugoslavia while bigger groups were transported to other camps.

The Vacant Seat

Once we were in the van, those with me were sure we were being taken back to Yugoslavia. Since there were no individual seats in the van but benches along the sides, the majority decided to start rocking and swaying in order to overturn the van in an attempt to escape. I pleaded with them not to, but they argued with me that it would be too late once we found ourselves in Sezana, a city just across the border in Yugoslavia.

After much pleading though, they gave up on the idea. The driver drove fast through the streets of Trieste. Prior to boarding the van I had asked a lady to whom I told about my faith and who came to the meetings with me in our church in Trieste to call our minister in Trieste and ask him to meet me at the railway station. She did as I asked, and while traveling in the van, I prayed I would see my brother in Christ at the railway station.

Finally, the van came to an abrupt stop. The back doors were opened, but like me, everyone was hesitant to come out. We were told we have arrived at the railway station, and to our great joy, it was not a lie. An officer told us to follow him. He led us to the platform, and we saw a sign for Rome. Then, and only then, did I feel a great burden fall off my chest. Finally, I was free.

My prayers had not been in vain. I was heading to the land of freedom, and I could not describe the feeling of joy I experienced. I felt as though I was floating on air.

As we walked along the platform, I was overjoyed to see a small group of my fellow believers waiting anxiously to see if I would arrive. When they saw me, they ran toward me with open arms as if we had not seen each other for a very long time, even though it had only been three days. We talked and cried at the same time. It was a time of joy and a time of sorrow because I was leaving them. Who knew when, if ever, we would meet again.

Somehow by now I seemed to have hardened to separations. I had been saying goodbye to so many people that I felt it was my lot in life to separate from those I loved. After spending an hour with them, it was time to board the train. They must have reserved the whole part of the wagon for us since we were all in the same section of the train, four to each compartment. I had no idea which country I would end up in. What I didn't know then was that it would be twenty years before I was to return to Europe.

As the train started moving, we waved frantically to each other. Some of the younger ones ran along the platform to see me for a little longer, even if it was just a few moments, but as the train gained speed, we lost contact, and I sat on my seat in the train that was taking me to Rome.

It was early morning when we arrived at the railway station in Rome. I had slept very little during the night. I felt as if I was seeing my life in some kind of film, showing the whole panorama of what I had been through in the previous two years.

My mind was also occupied by what was ahead of me. Finally, as the train stopped, it was announced that all passengers were to disembark. Again, an immigration officer came and led us to a bus that was waiting to take us to city of Latina, sixty kilometers south.

Chapter 16

Settling into the New Camp

The camp was situated on the outskirts of the city. It was vastly different from the one in Trieste. The buildings were clean, and the gardens were well kept with flowers and shrubs. There were clean paths and benches all along. It resembled more of a park than a refugee camp. There were buildings for families and for single people.

After all the formalities, we were taken to our rooms. I was placed in a room with about twenty other people. I was happy that my bed was again in the corner, as in the camp in Trieste. That gave me some privacy and provided a buffer from hearing people snoring on both sides. We were given clean bed linens and all the instructions regarding the camp order and timetables. We were told this would be our home until each one of us would migrate to the country where we would start a new life.

The meal times were issued, and I was once again faced with the problem of requesting vegetarian food. The next day after arriving I went to the dining room and asked the lady in charge if I could get food without meat. As it happened she was from Macedonia, a republic that at that time was part of Yugoslavia. She was understanding of my situation, but at the same time, she told me it was impossible to meet my request since there were thousands of people in this camp, and I was virtually the only person with such a request.

She then told me to go to the office and talk to the officer in charge; she also told me there was an interpreter, and I should have no problem communicating my request. This I did immediately. Once in the office a young man greeted me and asked me in Serbian if I needed any help. I told him my reason for coming. He then took me to the office of the man in charge of food supply. He was an Italian man of rather large proportions and surprisingly tall.

The young man told him my request, and after asking me a number of questions as to the reason for being vegetarian and how long I had been one, he told me they could not supply me with vegetarian meals but that he would give me a note and I could go to the lady in charge to whom I had talked with earlier. She would supply me with any food items I needed, and I could then prepare meals for myself. She would also give me fruit.

I was very thankful, and for the next five or so months that I stayed in the camp, I had a good supply of food. Here I experienced what it meant to be in a free country. I would have never been given this type of provision in my country, ruled by Communism.

The Vacant Seat

There was a family who were members of the SDA Church who I first met in the Trieste camp. There was a mother with four children, a daughter my age and three sons who were younger. I told them how I got food, and the mother told me that most of the meals actually contained clean meats, and they were lucky to be able to eat from the dining room.

One day the mother, as I called her by now, came to me crying. She had just discovered they had eaten horse meat, and she asked me to intervene for them to receive the raw food that she could cook herself. Since they were a family, they had been given a private room and the provision of the kitchen facilities with a cooking stove. I agreed to ask, but when I went, the Italian man was unwilling to do so, saying they had been eating from the dining room and should continue.

The mother began to cry, and I pleaded with the man again. Finally, he relented and gave her the same paper as he had given me. That was wonderful news, and she offered to cook for me also, so from that day onward, I brought my provisions to her and we ate together. I thanked God for the wonderful care of this dear family and me. Our friendship was close, and I was accepted as a member of their family, which helped fill the terrible void I felt in missing my own mother and brothers and sisters.

Chapter 17

Registration to Immigrate

All the camp residents were informed they must register in the consular office of the country they chose to immigrate to as there were many countries taking in immigrants. It was my firm intention to immigrate to the United States. The main reason for this decision was that I knew a very dear family from my village and church, the Satelmeir family, whose son Nicolaus was my good friend, who were in the States.

As soon as I made it to Italy I wrote them a letter informing them I had succeeded in leaving Yugoslavia. They replied while I was in the Trieste camp and sent me an official invitation to come to the United States and settle there.

In the Latina camp I went to the U.S. consular office, told the officer my intention to immigrate to the United States, and asked about registering. The officer was very kind and welcoming. After taking all my details, he told me to study English at the two English classes held daily in the camp. He further informed me it would take up to a year before I got my visa.

He assured me, however, that I need not worry. He said, "You will live in the United States and be free."

I thanked him, and when I exited the office, I felt as if I was living a pleasant dream. I thanked God that finally I would be able to serve Him in a free country.

After a short time I met other people and became friends with some of them. There were two or three young men my age or similar with whom I spent most of my day. There was also another man older than I who became very interested in the book I was reading.

Every day at a certain time I would sit on one of the benches and read my book. The book, of course, was my precious Bible that I had brought from Yugoslavia when I was escaping. I had decided to read the whole Bible during my stay in the camp.

This man, who was eleven years older than I, kept coming and sitting next to me. He would ask me questions about my beliefs and about the Bible. At first I was cautious about answering all of his questions. He noticed my hesitancy, and he assured me he was not a communist agent, but a migrant as I was. He told me he genuinely wanted to know more about my faith.

I told him every detail of the truth that I knew at that time. I told him about the Bible, which I believed was the Word of God. During the five months I was in the camp, I spoke to this man of the wonderful God I believed in and His Word, the Bible. I also enjoyed the company of my "new family" who I dined with, and the daughter became my close friend.

The Vacant Seat

Of the other people I met, I remained cautious because I was unsure exactly who they were. With those I became friends with, we spent our time walking around the camp, attending English classes, and from time to time going to town.

There was another good opportunity for me at the camp in regards to my trade. There was a workshop in the camp, and being a tailor, I was able to repair some clothing for my friends. We received clothes from the United Nations and other charitable organizations, and oftentimes the clothes didn't fit, but with a little work, I was able to fit them for my friends and myself.

After a while other people noticed I was working in the workshop and asked me to do repairs for them as well. Since nobody had much money, I asked them to just give as much as they could for my services. It was a very good opportunity for me to earn a little bit of money, and with that money I was able to buy suitable clothes. I also bought myself a suitcase and some food items I wasn't receiving in the camp.

During my few excursions to town, I began to learn the Italian language. When you are in Italy at the markets, you don't pay the price they ask, you have to bargain. I learned very quickly how to bargain. I must have become very good at it because very often I paid less than the price they were asking.

Among my friends we discussed our future and where we intended to live. I told them I was going to the United States. One of my friends asked me, "How long will you have to wait to migrate to the United States?"

I told him that it could take up to a year.

He then said to me, "Why stay here in the camp a whole year? Why don't you go to Australia? The Australian consul promises that within five months of registration you will be in Australia."

So I went to the Australian office and asked how long it would take to immigrate if I registered to go to Australia. The consul told me exactly as my friend had told me, five months. I could not believe what I was hearing. I told the consul I wanted to register. He responded reasonably and told me to sit down and tell him my details.

After taking all my information, he gave me a folder that contained information about Australia, and he welcomed me so warmly I felt as though I was already there. At the same time, however, I did not go to the American consul to cancel my registration. I decided I would go to whichever country called me first.

Life in the camp continued very much the same. Of course, all of us were impatient to go to the country of our designation to start our new life. As promised by the Australian consul, it was barely five months and I was called to the office. Once in the office I was told some good news.

"Mr. Jaksic, your documents are ready to go to Australia."

He handed me the documents and many other papers. Since I had no passport, they provided me with travel documents stamped with the Australian visa. The men wished me a good trip and told me that in two days I would be leaving for Australia.

I was so excited. I felt as if I was dreaming. After leaving the office, I told my friends and "family" at the camp the good news. Everybody was happy that I was finally going to Australia.

Registration to Immigrate

The next day I packed the few belongings I had and boarded the bus that took me to the city of Naples. Upon arrival in Naples, we were put up in a hotel overnight so that we would be ready to board the ship the next morning that would take us to Australia. Early the next morning an immigration officer woke us up and told us to pack and follow him to where the ship was waiting for us. As we boarded the ship, we were given cabins where we would sleep. We were also shown the dining room and other facilities.

The name of the ship was Neptunia, and it carried approximately 1,200 passengers on that voyage to Australia. Most of the passengers were Italians who were very emotional; many people cried as they said goodbye to their families. It was quite touching to witness this scene. I had no one to say goodbye to me since my family was in Yugoslavia and the friends I had made in the camp either came with me or stayed behind.

From Naples we journeyed to Genoa, another big port. From Genoa we traveled to Sicily. From Sicily we went to the Suez Canal. For the first four days of the journey I was very seasick and could hardly walk and eat. What comforted me was, if one could call it comfort, that there were many other people who were sick like me. After four days though, the sickness stopped.

Of all the passengers there were only twenty-five people from Yugoslavia, and since we could communicate among ourselves, the ship authorities arranged five tables where we could all sit together and talk. Quite often I would go on the upper deck and read my Bible. During one of the times I was reading, one of the Yugoslavian men came to me and very quickly told me to be careful what I talked about during mealtime. We would often discuss Yugoslavia and our life as we sat around the tables.

Of the twenty-five of us, I was the only Serbian national. The others were from Croatia and were Croatian nationals. I was not aware that these young men, who were similar in age to me, were poisoned by the Ustashi propaganda while in Italy. The Ustashi was a political party that during World War II was led by Ante Pavelic who was Hitler's puppet and fought on the side of Nazi Germany.

While we talked, they asked me about my background and my family. I told them I grew up in a village, attended school there, and learned my trade in Belgrade, at that time the capital city of Yugoslavia. When this young Croatian came to me, he looked around as if making sure no one saw us, and then he continued in virtually a whisper, "Be careful what you say at the table. They, the rest of them, suspect you to be a communist, and they are planning to throw you overboard." After saying this he quickly went away.

I was in a state of shock. Even here one was not safe. I prayed to God for protection from the evil intents of these people. From then on I spoke very little during the meals.

At the very beginning of the trip I met a nice family from Poland who were migrating to Australia. They talked to me quite often and invited me to sit with them at their table for meals since there were only three of them, a couple with their daughter who was about the same age as I.

After this kind friend told me of the danger I was in, I asked to be moved to the table with this family from Poland. Fortunately, my request was granted. This meant being saved from almost certain death. I kept away from them and never ventured to the deck by myself.

Chapter 18

Arriving in Australia

The journey to Australia took thirty days. We went through the Suez Canal and then headed straight for the Australian port of Fremantle in western Australia. Many of the passengers disembarked there, and after two days we continued our journey to Melbourne. While we were in Fremantle, we were able to get off the ship and visit the shops near the dock. Those who had money could even go into town.

As I stepped off the boat onto Australian soil for the first time, a strange feeling came over me and questions flooded my mind. Is this my new home? How will it be? Where will I live? Where will I work? Endless thoughts swirled in my head. At the same time I was overwhelmed with the heat; it was unbearably hot. If Australia is always like this, how can I live here? Those of us who had just arrived from Europe were not used to the hot climate.

As we continued our journey to Melbourne, the sea grew rough and the waves were high. Many people became sick. Fortunately, I was not affected, and we finally entered the Melbourne port. Before we disembarked, an officer from the Immigration Department came on board. Those of us who had no one to meet were told we would journey by train to a refugee camp.

I was perplexed finding out Australia had such camps. The immigration officer told us of the procedures we were to follow and called us one by one by our surnames. As we approached him he attached a number to our clothes. This was another shock. A number—I was now known or identified by a number. This was difficult to accept to say the least. Furthermore, he told us we could not lose this number as this was how they would identify us until we arrived at the camp, which was a full days travel by train.

The trip to the camp in Bonegilla took all day by train. While on the train, the officers in charge asked if any of us spoke English. I put my hand up and said I could say some a few words I had learned while in the camp in Italy. Again, they placed me in the same compartment in the train as my Croatian "friends" who did not understand a word in English. It was my job to explain to them the stations the train would stop at, how long it would be there, and the meal times along the journey. They made no comments, but they listened quietly as I spoke in my Serbian accent.

They were not aware I knew of their plot while on the ship. My true Croatian friend was among them. Finally, toward late evening we arrived at our destination. Once in the camp they issued us sheets and took us to our rooms where we would sleep during our stay in the camp. They gave us timetables for meals and told us we had to be on time for meals or we would not eat.

They allocated me a room with two other people. To begin with though there was just two of us in the room, a young man from Germany and me. After a few days the man who had been with me in the Latina camp to whom I spoke to about my faith arrived at the camp. Soon after his arrival he inquired as to my whereabouts. He was told which room I was in, and he asked if he could stay in the same room. He was told he could since there were only two of us and there were three beds in the room. I was surprised when I saw him and at the same time happy, especially because I was able to talk to him so much about my faith, which I felt he was genuinely interested in.

He was happy to see me also and told me we would have much to talk about. He settled in to the vacant bed. We talked late into the night about what had transpired since we parted in Italy, and we talked about our trip to Australia. We had much in common since we both were from Serbia, but to me nationality never mattered, what mattered was the kind of person someone was and how one related as a human being.

The next day we talked more, and he told me he wanted to see some of his friends he had met while in the camp in Italy. At the same time, I found some of my friends I had also met in Italy. There was another young man my age who was Catholic. I also had the privilege of sharing my faith with him. He was a good friend, and we spent many hours discussing our beliefs and other issues. We had very little money other than what the camp authorities gave us for our personal needs, but we didn't have enough money to buy clothes or any items that were more costly.

Then an opportunity arose to earn some money. One morning we heard the announcement that pickers were needed for the pear harvest. All who were interested should report to the office. When I heard this, I did not delay in going to the office to register. Within two days a group of us were on our way to the largest pear plantation I had ever seen. We traveled by bus all day before reaching the farm. Once there we were given accommodations very similar to that in the camp. There were four per room: myself, my Catholic friend Marco, and another man about our age. One bed was still vacant. After two days my Serbian friend arrived and took the fourth bed.

We were again together, as in Italy, and we felt good that we could be together in this far away country where we did not know anyone else. The farmer provided our meals, and once again I was faced with the fact that I was a vegetarian. I shared that with the farmer, and he asked me if I ate eggs and dairy products, to which I replied that I did. I have never eaten so many eggs in my life, not until then, nor since. For every meal I found eggs on my plate. They were boiled, fried, poached, scrambled, or prepared in any way the cook invented.

After breakfast we all were taken to the plantation to pick pears. At first the work was very hard for me. We were all given a bag with a handle that went over our shoulder. The bag was designed with flaps so that when you filled the bag with pears you just undid the buttons and slowly poured the pears into the trailer.

The Vacant Seat

For the first few days the muscles in my arms, legs, and back were very sore. For lunchtime we were taken back to the house, and after an hour we had to go back to pick pears. After a few days I started to feel a lot better. I have never eaten so many pears in my life. There were some very beautiful ripe pears that were very sweet, and we were told that while pouring them into the trailer we had to be very careful and not bruise them.

Prior to coming to the farm to pick pears, I had written a letter to our church headquarters in Sydney asking them to send me an invitation as that would be the only way to get out of the camp.

While at the farm a letter arrived from Sydney. I realized it was the invitation. I showed it to the farmer and told him I wanted to go back to the camp and then from the camp to Sydney. After showing him the letter, he told me I had to wait a few days until more people planned to go back to the camp so the bus would be full.

Finally the time came for me to leave the farm. I felt good. I had money in my pocket, and I was going to Sydney. Once back in the camp, arrangements were made for me and two other men to travel to Sydney by train. We were given tickets and other documents. We first traveled from the camp to Melbourne and then to Sydney by overnight train.

We arrived at the Sydney central railway station early in the morning. There was no one to meet us at the station. After making a few inquiries, I bought a ticket for a train to take me to the suburb of Summer Hill. I had the address of our church headquarters. I walked to 42 Prospect Road. As I arrived there I saw the big sign showing the name of our church. I read the sign but went past, then returned, reading the sign again. As I was reading the sign the people in the office noticed me. After seeing me, one of the ministers, Brother Weymark, came out to meet me. He spoke to me in English and invited me in.

He told me he had seen me reading the sign and had guessed it was the young man who had written from the Bonegilla camp. And he was right. I was young, just twenty-one years of age, almost six foot tall, and I was very slim, weighing about fifty-five kilograms. But I was healthy and that was important.

Once in the front office, his father and wife welcomed me very warmly. I was tired from my overnight trip. They showed me the bathroom, and I took a shower. After that they fed me a delicious meal. I was then shown to the room where I could rest, and before long, I was fast asleep. I woke up around 4:30 in the afternoon. I was given another meal and then Brother Weymark took me to see a family who had come from Yugoslavia three years earlier. Unfortunately, they had no accommodations for me since they already had two young men living with them, one of whom I knew from Belgrade. But they suggested to Brother Weymark to take me to the Risko family. We traveled by train, which was a new experience for me as I had never traveled in the city by train. There are no such things in Yugoslavia.

Once at the Risko's we were warmly received, and they told me I could board with them for five pounds a week in their upstairs room.

Chapter 19

My First Job in Australia

The next day Sister Risko took me to a wire factory that was just around the corner from their house. I got a job, and the supervisor showed me what I would be doing. It was a Monday in February 1960, and I was to start work the next Monday.

On Tuesday morning I told Sister Risko I wanted to go to the city to look for a job as a tailor. She asked me how I could do this since I spoke very little English and did not know my way around the city. I asked her to tell me where the station was, and I would go by train.

After giving me directions and letting me know which station to get off of, I left. After boarding a train, I traveled to Sydney, an experience I will never forget. I still remember riding through the city streets and seeing all of the advertising signs posted along the way. One large sign read, "What we eat today walks and talks tomorrow." At the time I could not comprehend what they were trying to say, but years later I understood the message. Another sign read, "Help us to help others."

I saw many backyards, washing lines, and fences between the back gardens. Some were neat and clean, others were full of junk. Some were small houses, some big with swimming pools in the backyard.

After Central Station the train went underground, and the lights came on in the train. All this was new to me, and I felt as if I was in some dreamland. After Town Hall station, we arrived at Wynyard Station. I got off here and followed the crowd of passengers exiting the train. I didn't know it at the time, but Sydney would be my home for eleven years and would be where I would meet a very lovely woman who would later become my wife. In addition, it would be the place I would go to church and a place where my first son would be born.

As I got off the train I did not ask anyone for any directions. I did not know exactly where I was going, and I knew I would not understand what anyone said. After walking for a while, I found myself on Pitt Street. It was the center of the city. There were many shops, mostly clothing shops for women. Then I saw a very nice shop with men's suits displayed in the window. I read the big sign above the window: HOUSE and HOUSE. I thought this would be a nice place to work in.

Gaining courage, I walked in. The man who served asked me a question I did not understand. He then repeated it, asking me if I wanted something, if he could help me. Then I understood. I told him, "Yes, I am looking for a position." I had read these words in the dictionary, so I repeated what I thought

The Vacant Seat

was the best way to describe wanting a job. He then asked me if I was looking for a job.

"Yes," I said. "I want a position."

"Okay," he said, "come with me."

He took me downstairs to a large room that was a workshop with many people working there. The man, who I later learned was a supervisor, was very friendly and showed me around the workshop. He asked me if I could do the work, and I nodded.

He took me to a big pressing machine, where a man was working and asked if I could work the machine. I said no as I had never seen that kind of press. He said it would be no problem and asked me when I could start. I said Monday.

He wrote down my name and address, and as I was about to leave, he shook hands with me and said, "See you on Monday at 7:30 a.m."

I was very excited as I walked out of the shop. I had my first job in Australia. What made it so good was that I had found the job myself, and I would be working in my trade as a tailor.

When I got back home, I told Sister Risko I had found a job as a tailor and I would be starting on Monday. She gasped in disbelief, but she, of course, was happy for me.

Brother Risko was a boot maker with his own shop. On Wednesday night he took me to church for prayer meeting where I met a number of church people. Among them was Brother Kraus. When he went home after the meeting, his sister Christine and his cousin Mary asked him if there was any news. He told them, "Yes, a young man came from Yugoslavia, and he is a tailor."

On Thursday he asked me if I had a Sabbath suit and other clothes. I showed him the few clothes I had in my little suitcase. He then offered to take me to the city to choose a suit, shirt, shoes, and other items of clothing I needed. He agreed to pay for them until I earned enough money to pay him back.

I was moved by his kindness, and I gladly accepted his offer. He took me to some nice shops where I chose a good suit. Being a tailor, I chose well. It was expensive, but he said nothing; he just paid for it. It was the same for the shoes, shirt, socks, underwear, and other items.

We arrived home with a number of parcels. I cannot explain the feeling of joy I had. I had just arrived in my new home country, and I was being shown such wonderful kindness. I determined that if someday I was in the position to help as Brother Risko helped me I was going to do the same for those in need. Thank God, my desire was fulfilled, and I have been given a number opportunities over the years to help those in need.

When I went to church on Sabbath, a beautiful young woman called Mary, who wore white gloves, extended her right hand to greet me. She welcomed me with the most wonderful smile I had ever received. It had a tremendous impact on me—a smile I have never forgotten to this day. Later at home she commented to her family that it was obvious I was a tailor by the nice suit I wore.

Three years later, this beautiful woman became my wife.

Chapter 20

Meeting Old Friends

My great joy after arriving in Sydney was meeting my friends Joseph and Vasa Dimitrijevic who I knew from Yugoslavia. Joseph had been with me when I had made my second attempt to escape from Yugoslavia. I hadn't seen him since we were caught and imprisoned, so it was a wonderful reunion. We had much to talk about, in particular our adventures since we had been separated.

I was fortunate I had found a job, and as such, I sent money to my mother in Yugoslavia who was still struggling to keep my two younger sisters at home. She had no support from our father, and at that time there were no government operated social security programs in Yugoslavia, so a mother with small children and no husband or any means of financial support practically starved to death.

Fortunately, my mother had land, and she grew vegetables and other crops that provided them with food, but there was no money for clothes or other necessities, so I sent her enough money every month to pay the bills.

After two months at my job, I read in the employment column in the newspaper about a job for a hand tailor. This was what I was looking for as I had been trained in Belgrade as a hand tailor. This was a perfect opportunity for me to get back to my real trade. After work I went to the address in the ad, and I found that the shop made suits the same way I had been trained in Belgrade. The job suited me very well, and after a short interview, I was asked when I could start.

After giving a week's notice to my employer, I started at my new job. It was good and I loved it. There were just four of us. The owner was a master tailor, a Jewish man from Poland who survived the Holocaust. There was also a lady who was the finisher and another tailor the same as I. I worked there for seven months. My boss liked the way I worked, and I was happy in the shop, but the pay was not very good. At that time the Australian currency was the pound. He was paying me twelve pounds per week to start with, but not knowing what the actual weekly salary was, I accepted it without any question. Out of that I had to pay five pounds board and travel to work, plus other expenses, which did not leave me much to save or send to my mother.

My friends told me he should pay me at least sixteen pounds per week. I approached him about it, but he declined. After working for seven months, he increased my pay by three pounds, but it was still not enough, so I looked in the papers for a better paying job.

The Vacant Seat

I was fortunate to find other employment, and I went to work for a firm that did manufacturing, mostly by machine. I realized I needed to earn more, and hand tailoring was a dying art. Within one year I changed jobs three times, but each one was a change for the better.

One day Mary asked me if I was happy where I worked, and she suggested I try to get a job where she worked. It was a big company, and she said the conditions were very good. The next day I took a day off from work and went to the factory where she worked. The factory was in St. Marys in Sydney's west end, so I had to travel a fair distance.

What I didn't know at the time was that this job would change the direction of my life.

Before even coming to Australia, it had been my intention to continue my education. I planned to study English and then go to school and on to university. When I started life in Australia, I soon realized I had to work to earn my own living, but it did not stop me from studying English for a year by attending evening classes funded by the Australian government in a local school. I loved going to the classes, and it helped me to communicate better.

When I went for the interview at the big factory, the personnel woman must have liked what I told her about my experience, for she asked me to start as soon as possible. I told her I could start in a week, and she called the cutting department manager, a tall suave Englishman with a strong English accent, and asked him to take me to the cutting room and show me the workflow. He told me I would only be cutting while the others would be marking for me, but he informed me that after a while I could mark my own work. The pay was much better than any other job I had had.

It was a good move, and I was very thankful to Mary for the suggestion to try to get a job there. The factory was none other than Anthony Squires, one of the most popular clothing factories in Australia. As I went back to my little place, I realized that I needed to find a place closer to my work. I had saved some money from my previous jobs, so I bought an old house by paying a 10 percent deposit. I was able to move in soon after that.

Chapter 21

Buying My First House

I bought the house from one of our church ministers who was being transferred to Queensland. The minister had to leave as soon as possible. For me it was a historic move in Australia. After one year in my new country I had gone from nothing to owning a home of my own, which I paid off in eight years.

I cannot describe the feelings I had when I moved in and spent my first night in my new home. I was so excited I could not sleep. I had followed the instructions of my mother who had told me to avoid renting. She told me to buy a place as soon as I could, no matter how humble it may be. And humble it was.

It was made from timber, and the walls were asbestos, known as a fibro cottage. In the 1960s and 1970s thousands if not hundreds of thousands of such houses were built to accommodate the influx of migrants who could not afford anything better. This was indeed a wonderful opportunity for people like me to live in their own house.

It needed a lot of repairs and painting, but I was happy, and in time all was fixed. It was nice to go home after work and do some repairs around the house and tend to the garden where I planted some vegetables. The job was going well, and I enjoyed my work.

After about a year in Australia, my younger sister Mira came from Yugoslavia and married a man named Paul who was from our church. It proved to be an unfortunate union, and the marriage ended in divorce. They had one son Robert, her pride and joy, who made my sister's life meaningful. Years later my mother also migrated to Australia with my youngest sister, Milena. It was good to have them with me, as I no longer felt so isolated. Now half my family was in Australia and half in Yugoslavia.

After about two years in Australia, I decided it was time for me to start thinking about marriage. While still in Yugoslavia, I met a girl in our church I liked very much, and all this time I had been corresponding with her.

I was now ready to take the big step and get married. I wrote to her of my plans, and she insisted I come back to Yugoslavia for the wedding. It was an impossible request. I could not go back because I had left the country illegally, and because of the military call up, I was regarded as a soldier. If I went back I would be arrested on arrival and sentenced to nine years in prison.

The Vacant Seat

I tried to explain all this to her, but she insisted upon me returning to Yugoslavia. After long negotiations, it was evident we disagreed on more than one point, and we parted ways. With my sweetheart from Yugoslavia out of the picture, I started having serious thoughts about Mary.

My friends told me, "You don't have a chance. Don't even try."

I thought my friends were wrong, so I tried anyway. I had a wonderful advantage and opportunity to spend time together because we traveled forty-five minutes to work every day by train, so we had plenty of time to talk and get to know each other.

Chapter 22

Getting Serious About Marriage

After my failed attempt at marrying the girl back home, I began to court Mary, but I was cautious, since my friends insisted I would suffer great disappointment. As time went on, we became more and more friendly, and I felt real love for her. I realized I wanted to be with her for the rest of my life. There was something different about her. Her smile and her dignified bearing of honesty and faithfulness to a God she believed in captivated me. I decided to make every effort to win her heart.

To the surprise of my friends, Mary and I became serious about our future. My sister Mira at first thought it was all in fun, but she too realized we were serious based on the frequent visits I made to the Kraus family. One day she asked me if I wanted to marry Mary.

"Yes, I intend to marry her," I said.

"Did you ask her?" my sister said.

"Not yet."

"What if she says no? What will you do then?"

I told her to leave it to me. I realized that there was a possibility she would say no. My close friend and some other young men in our church were also interested in her.

I kept in constant contact with her, and I prayed that if it was God's will she would be my wife. At least three to four times a week I would ride to her home on my old bicycle, which was all I could afford for transportation. She lived with her three cousins not far from my house. On one occasion as I was riding to see her, a dog attacked me. As much as I tried to kick him off, he was very persistent, and he bit me badly, ripping a piece of flesh off my leg.

A group of people who were standing on the street talking saw the attack but did not try to stop the dog from biting me. I stopped and said, "Your dog just bit me very badly."

Their reaction was a loud laugh. I tried to stop the bleeding by tying my sock around the wound. Patched up as best I could, I continued on my way to see my sweetheart. My conclusion was that I needed to suffer some inconvenience for my love. Fortunately, the wound healed nicely.

The Vacant Seat

Mary and I had been courting for about one year when I decided to "take the plunge," as the saying goes. I thought carefully about how I would ask her. I was shy, poor, and not very experienced with matters of romance. I had a permanent job, and I had paid a deposit for the old house I now lived in. We both worked at the same company, and it was a good place to work, particularly as I had good prospects to advance to management level.

Presently I worked as a cutter, but my boss was asking me if I would be willing to move to a more satisfying job that would give me better pay. I told him I was willing to accept any challenge.

My time with Mary intensified. We spent countless hours together discussing various aspects of life, marriage, family, children, and work. Some of my friends tried their best to discourage me from pursuing anything further with her, but I told them not to worry.

The day finally came when I decided the sun was not going to set before I asked the all-important question. As we walked to the front gate, I said, "Would you like to be my special friend?"

Her answer was affirmative. "Yes!"

I flew home so fast on my bike that no dog could have ever caught me, not even a greyhound. As I sat in my home, I thought how foolish and stupid I had been. I should have asked her if she would be my wife, not just my special friend.

First I was angry with myself, but then I decided I would ask her the question later. This time I would say, "I would love for you to be my wife. Will you marry me?"

The day had been good. My prospects seemed bright on many fronts, so I decided to make things official on another day.

Shortly thereafter on the way home from work one day I asked Mary if she was free that evening. She said she was, and after arriving at home, I got ready, got on my old faithful bicycle, and pedaled to her place. I flew, dogs or no dogs; nothing could stop me now. That day had to be the day.

Upon arriving, I started feeling a little nervous, but my determination was firm. After accepting a drink, I asked her if she would go out with me, and she accepted. Of course as I had no car, we had to walk to the railway station to catch a train to the city. Once there we went to a nice park, and then I summoned up the greatest courage of my life.

"Mary, my dear, will you marry me? I would love to share the rest of my life with you. I love you."

She was stunned to say the least. After a few moments that seemed like an eternity, she looked at me, and then both of us stretched out our arms and embraced each other. We held each other for a long time, and she whispered, "Yes, yes I too want to spend the rest of my life with you."

That evening we both walked on air. At least I know I did.

Now we had the serious business of preparing for the big day. I was advised we should announce our engagement in church. I was not aware of this as it was not the custom in my village, but it was no

Getting Serious About Marriage

problem. Nothing was too hard to do as long as things were moving closer to the moment when we would be together.

We made plans to announce that our wedding would take place on March 10, 1963. We had no parents with us as they were still in Europe, and it was not possible for them to come, so we had to make all the preparations ourselves. We approached Pastor Weymark and asked him to officiate at the service. We also asked Pastor Stewart and Pastor Haynes, who were of the old school, to assist with the wedding ceremony. They gave us some strict guidelines as to how our wedding should be conducted.

For me anything was acceptable as long as they did not tell me Mary could not be my wife, but they commended me on choosing this wonderful and faithful woman as my helpmate. After a lot of preparation, the only thing left was to make our wedding garments. Mary made her own dress—I helped a little bit—and I made my suit, or I should say I closely followed the process as it was being made at the company I worked for.

March 10 approached quickly, and the preparations continued to go smoothly. Mary was more in control than I was; I had very little or no experience about wedding customs in Australia. She had good advisers in her friends Mr. and Mrs. Jeffs who virtually adopted her and acted as her parents.

Mira was the only one I had from my side of the family, while Mary had her cousins John, Maria, and Christine.

Finally the big day arrived. The evening before the wedding, I spent the night with Brother and Sister Brus, while Mary stayed with the Jeffs. Brother Brus was my driver while Mr. Jeffs drove Mary in his black Holden car. My good friend Joseph, who'd been with me on my second escape attempt from Yugoslavia, was my best man.

The ceremony at church went well, although I was so anxious I don't remember much of it. I just held onto Mary and made sure she was near me. After it was over, we all went to the reception hall where we ate the wedding breakfast. That expression was new to me, but I didn't care what they called it; Mary was my wife, and that was all that mattered.

After breakfast there was the customary cutting of the wedding cake and the speeches and other trivia. Then we said goodbye to all the guests and left for our secret honeymoon destination. It was none other than my house, where Mary had moved in her furniture during the week before the wedding.

The Vacant Seat

The only people who knew our secret honeymoon destination were Joseph and Mr. Jeffs. Joseph had the key to the house and had packed up all the wedding presents and took them there. Mr. Jeffs drove us to our place, and we sped off in the back seat, waving to all.

As we arrived at our home, Mr. Jeffs wished us all the best. We thanked him and he left. It was late, but I did not feel tired. I was on top of the world. Mary was my wife!

As I looked for the key where Joseph should have left it, it was not there. I looked all over the place but in vain. The only way other option was to see if the bedroom window would open. We were fortunate that it opened, but I had to carry my bride over the threshold into my house through the window. With a little help, she landed safely, and I soon followed.

But there was now an even a bigger problem—the bedroom door was locked. That meant we had to go out through the window and try other windows to gain access to the rest of the house.

Originally thinking we were away, Joseph decided to come late in the afternoon the next day. He was surprised to find us at home; then he realized he still had the keys to the house.

After about a week at home, we went to visit our friends in a place called Cooranbong where they had an outbuilding their sons named "Home Sweet Home." We spent a few days there, but money was limited, and we had to be content with what we had.

About two weeks later we went back to work, and life fell into a routine, which was wonderful.

Because we had no car, we had to use public transportation, but we were very happy. I painted and did some repairs around the house, and we established a nice garden with vegetables and many flowers. We went everywhere together whether it was to work, shopping, church, or visiting relatives or friends. It was wonderful bliss. I had no idea life could be so good. At work I continued to advance, and with each little advance my pay increased. It helped a lot as eighteen months later our precious little son Alexander Harold was born.

In those days fathers were not allowed to be present at the birth, so just before the baby was about to be born, I was sent out of the room. We didn't know whether it would be a boy or a girl until the birth.

Finally, someone emerged from the room and told me, "Mr. Jaksic, you are the proud father of a baby boy."

I could not restrain myself. I yelled at the top of my voice, "I have a son, I have a son!"

I couldn't wait to see my son. In the nursery I saw a little cot with a blue card and the name "JAKSIC" written on it. Another little Jaksic had come into the world. To me, newborn babies looked strange, and when I saw Mary after seeing my son, I asked her if he was all right. With strong assurance and calm, she told me he was perfect.

When Mary and our little bundle came home, we became a family of three. Mary busied herself in the house and with our little Alex. I went to work aware that I now had more responsibility than when I was single. But I felt happier than ever, and every day I looked forward to going home after work.

Chapter 23

Promotions at Work

At work, things were going well. The cutting room manager made me an offer that surprised me and made me somewhat apprehensive. The company employed 1,800 people, but with the prospects of growth within the company, they were selecting twenty-five to send to college—and I was one of the ones selected. But I could not understand why they picked me out of so many people who were born and educated in Australia and who were fluent in English. Those selected would study factory management and human relations for two years and then the successful graduates would be given jobs with more responsibility.

I felt honored and at the same time inadequate since my command of English was not up to the standard required. My manager's reply was that my English was the least of the company's concern. "You will learn as you go," he assured me.

I accepted the offer and soon started attending evening lectures at Penrith Technical College—books, transportation, and all expenses were paid for by the company. From time to time I had to attend lectures during the day, which meant being away from work, but they paid for those hours also. The first year I studied factory management, and the second year we covered human relations. I thoroughly enjoyed being at the college; it gave me valuable understanding of how industries work and the way management should perform and relate to their work and to the staff.

The second year was even more interesting. The human relations studies proved to be of great benefit for me in the industry, and as a side benefit, for when I started working in the church and dealing with the many situations of human nature. At the end of the two years, I sat for the final exams. I was nervous for a number of reasons.

Firstly, the company paid all my expenses, and I had to prove that they did not fail in choosing me. Secondly, I struggled with the English language throughout the two years of school, working extra hours just to understand what I was reading.

The exams were distributed, and we waited for the examining officer to give us the signal to start. We had three hours to complete the test, and all we had in our hands was the exam and a pen. At the end of the exam, we handed our papers back, and although I thought I did reasonably well, I was apprehensive as to the results that were to be sent to the company. Depending on the success of our tests, we would be offered management positions within the company. They would publish the results in the daily papers. I waited eagerly to see if I had passed, not expecting any high result.

Promotions at Work

We all eagerly waited for the Sydney Daily Telegraph and the results. We were graded A, B, C, and F if we failed. When the results finally came out, to my great surprise, I had passed with a B. That result was astonishing for me. My friend Merv, who was born and educated in Australia, passed with a C, and the son of the outgoing quality manager got an F.

He had spent two years with me in the same classes and never greeted me despite my attempts to greet him. He seemed to think he was somewhat superior. He worked in the office and preferred to mix and talk with those who were of the same class as he. We, the workers, especially those of us with strong European accents, did not count for much to him.

Not long after the company received the results, I was offered a job that would give me better conditions and an increase in earnings. I was to be on quality inspection in the cutting room. Some of the cutters were put on piecework because they were careless in their work and the quality suffered. I had to make sure the high standard in the cutting room was sustained. This brought me into conflict with some of the cutters, but despite this I tried to maintain good relationships with most of them and do the work the company required of me.

After working in that job for about a year, and after a period of training under the outgoing manager, I was offered the position of quality manager. Being only twenty-eight years of age, this posed a tremendous challenge for me as I felt it was too big a responsibility. But when the management made me the offer, I accepted and decided to see how it would go.

One problem arose almost at the start. The business dinners organized by the company where all the managers and supervisors would meet for a gourmet meal and discuss the issues arising in production, quality, and process were held on Friday nights.

When they asked if it would be okay with me, I had to tell them Friday nights would be out of the question because of the Sabbath. The managers were all Jewish, so they knew what I was talking about.

I then told them I would prefer to go back to being a cutter for a smaller salary than be a manager and break the holy Sabbath. They told me they would consider what I had said and would inform me of their decision in two days.

However, they did not wait for two days. The next day they told me they still wanted me to be in charge of quality and would change the business dinners from Friday to Thursday night, which surprised me.

As they were talking to me, one of the owners said, "Branko, you have good faith. I wish I had the same as you."

I then told him, "You can have the same faith, just determine to serve the God of your fathers, and He will give you strength."

It was a wonderful challenge for me, but at the same time, it was a great blessing to work with these good people, to be able to witness to them, and by the Lord's grace, to exceed management's expectations by producing higher quality garments.

The Lord was good to me and to us as a young family.

Chapter 24

The Call to Work for the Lord

In 1970 the Australasian Union Conference Session was held, and I attended the evening public meetings. I was not a delegate, but I was greatly surprised when they asked me to come to the nominating committee. They told me the brethren were planning to expand the work in Australia. We had churches in every major city except Adelaide, and the plan was to take the message there. I told the brethren it was a very good plan.

Then they told me they were intending to send someone to work there. That too was a good plan. Then I asked, "Do you have someone to send there? Adelaide is 1,500 kilometers from Sydney, a long way for anyone living in Sydney."

The answer was, "Yes, we think we have someone to send."

"Who is it?" I asked, thinking they wanted my thoughts about that "someone." The answer they gave caused me to almost faint.

"It is you, dear brother. We would like you to move to Adelaide with your family."

"NO, NO!" I instantly replied.

I was not a Bible worker, although I did what I called private Bible work by studying with one family who by now was attending our church. I was also visiting a sister who lived in Canberra with six children. Mary and I went there every five weeks at our own expense as volunteers. That was all. Nothing compared to the full time work and study with people every day. I was devoted to my work with the company, and I loved it.

As it was evening, the brethren told me to think and pray overnight and to let them know in the morning. As I walked home and entered our bedroom, I was in sheer agony. Mary and our precious boy were asleep when I went in. I lay on the bed and prayed earnestly for some comfort from the Lord, but nothing came. Then a thought came to me, My wife will say no. I could not even imagine she would be willing to move that far from the church and our family, and that would be my answer to the brethren.

The Call to Work for the Lord

Despite this solution, I could not sleep. Early in the morning, I told Mary what the brethren had asked me.

"They want us to move to Adelaide, 1,500 kilometers from here, to leave my good job, to leave our relatives and all the brethren and sisters here, and to start work in Adelaide. It's not possible," I told her. "But I must ask you. Do you want to go?"

Her answer shocked me. "If we believe this is the truth that the Lord wants us to proclaim, then we should go."

"And are you prepared to leave all our people and my good job and go to the desert?" I was perplexed and concerned.

We talked further and made up our minds. When the time came, I went to the nominating committee and told them we would go.

I was a staff member and had to resign from the company with three months notice. At the end of three months, the management and all the staff wished me well. As they told me goodbye, the general manager said, "Brian"—that was the name they called me—"the doors of this company are always open for you, and if things do not go well for you in Adelaide, you can come back."

For me this was comforting assurance. Thank the Lord it did not eventuate.

We sold our house in Sydney, as well as a parcel of land where we had planned to build ourselves a new dream home. We had already drawn plans up for our new house when the call came to go to Adelaide. It was difficult to part with that land as it was in a good area among very nice houses, but now we had to sell everything we had and move to Adelaide.

Chapter 25

A New Start

Because we did not have our own house in Adelaide, we had to rent. We finally bought land in a nice area, and after thirteen months we moved in to our newly built home.

The Lord was with us from the very start of our work. We worked and met many people in a relatively short time. We had many wonderful experiences that if I was to write about them all I would have to write another book. One particular experience saw the Lord bring a wonderful harvest.

In South Australia law forbids door-to-door selling on Sundays. That was the day I would normally spend four hours offering books to people and asking for donations. One particular Sunday I decided to work my normal four hours. I started at 10 a.m., chose the area of work, and started knocking on doors. The first hour passed with no responses. Most of the people opened their door enough just to show their face, and when I told them my reason for knocking, they would say, "No thank you, not today." Some did not even listen to the end of my presentation.

I thought I had at least another three hours, and from previous experiences, the second hour was always better. The second hour passed, and those who opened their doors said, "No thank you, not today." Then the third and fourth hour passed the same. By then I was tired as it was a very hot day, and I did not take any water with me. I was very thirsty and feeling hungry.

I told Mary I would be back at home by 2 p.m. After four hours without any results, I decided to visit homes for one more hour. But it was the same response. That had never happened before. Normally after one hour I would be able to start a number of conversations with people or generate some sales. I continued knocking, asking the Lord to show me what I was doing wrong. After another hour, I experienced the same results. By now I was getting very tired, but something kept telling me to keep going, and so I entered the seventh hour of knocking on doors without any results.

I decided to finish my marathon walk at the end of the street I was on, and when I finally came to the last house, I knocked and heard steps coming to the door. As the door opened, a rather fine woman appeared and asked me what I wanted.

After telling her my mission and showing her my books, she took one of the health books, glanced at it briefly and said, "No thank you, I have better books then this."

I was not going to let her go that easy. After seven hours of walking, she was the first person I had really talked to, and I asked her if I could see her books. She said yes and brought me one of them. Realizing it was an SDA publication, I asked her if she was an Adventist.

"Yes, I am," she said.

Because of the meeting with this woman at the end of my seven-hour walk, just over a year later there were nine souls baptized in our church. From the baptism came a wonderful blessing to the church in Australia as a whole. Directly from those who were baptized, today there are two ordained ministers, one ordained elder, three Bible workers, three field leaders, and a president of the Australasian Union. By the grace of the Lord, more souls were added to the fold as time went on. Today we have a nice church building filled with very wonderful people.

We arrived to Adelaide in July 1971, and in November of the same year, our second son, Wilfrid Jonathan, was born. It was a wonderful event but of course with it came greater responsibility. I felt greatly privileged to have two sons bearing my name—Jaksic. Two years later our sweet daughter, Esther, was born, and our family was complete.

When I arrived in Australia, I was single and had nothing. Thirteen years later I was a family man with a wife and three children. I felt on top of the world.

As far as the rest of our family was concerned, while in Sydney my wife's parents lived with us for three years. They were a great help but returned to Austria before we moved to Adelaide. My mother was in Australia for fifteen years and lived with me and with my two sisters in Sydney and in New Zealand. She too returned to her roots, going back to Yugoslavia where she built a church with the money she saved while in Australia.

Chapter 26

Children's Upbringing and Education

All parents do their best to raise their children to be well-rounded individuals, and we were no exception. As our children were growing up we endeavored to take particular care of their health, both physical and spiritual. Being vegetarians, we ensured they received the most nutritious foods to help their body and mind grow in the best possible way. They grew well physically and mentally. We also made sure they felt well cared for and loved.

We prayed and took them with us to church. As they grew they took an active part in church youth activities. It was also our aim to give them the best possible education, and as we did not have means to send them to private schools, we enrolled them in the public education system. They excelled in all the subjects from their first year to their twelfth year, graduating with top marks.

I recall when my employer (at that time I worked in my trade because of a lack of money in the union) who had two sons of similar age to our children, told me proudly that his oldest son had entered the Westpac mathematics competition. Those competitions were indeed highly competitive. They were held annually across Australia, and students from all schools, private and public, took the same tests. They simply had to be good to enter and to pass.

Of course it was almost a foregone conclusion and expectation that students from private education systems would perform much better. There may have been some truth in that since the students were highly motivated by the teaching staff not only to enter the competitions but to perform well. Similar training went on in public systems; however, it was up to the individual students to be self-motivated to enter and do their best to achieve the best results.

All three of my children entered the competitions on a regular basis. It was soon after the results were published that my employer came to me and said, "Brian, my son got a wonderful result in the Westpac math competition, and my wife and I are so proud of him."

Without waiting for me to ask what mark he got, he told me that he had received a "B."

My response was that that was a wonderful mark and if he continued that way, he would do well in life. Both of my employer's sons attended top private schools.

He then asked, "Did any of your children enter that competition?"

"Yes, all three of them entered," I said.

"Oh," he said. "They are ambitious, aren't they?"

"I guess they are," I said.

"Do many students from public schools enter those competitions?"

"I'm not sure, but mine enter every year."

"And how did they go, considering they had to compete against the students from the top private schools?"

Now came the moment that made me feel rather uncomfortable, but I had to tell the truth. I took a few moments before answering, but when I did the answer shocked him almost to the point of him losing his balance off the comfortable chair he was sitting on.

I said, "All three of them got 'A' marks."

He knew these were the top marks. With that, he turned around and told me it was time to start work since we had a very busy day ahead of us.

Years later, now that they are all professionals, people often ask me, "How did they, all three of them, become medical practitioners?"

I am at a loss to readily answer. To be admitted into medical school in Australia, you have to graduate from high school or college with the highest marks, and even that does not guarantee you entrance to study medicine.

When our oldest son, Alex, a straight-A student from the beginning to the end of his school years, had to decide what

The Vacant Seat

career path to pursue, my thoughts were that he should study agriculture as his skills would benefit the community as a whole. He, however, wanted to be a dentist. When completing the entrance application, he had to submit four or five different career options. He put dentistry as number one, then medicine, and three more. He then showed me the list.

After seeing the list, I casually commented, "If you want to spend your life looking in people's mouths, be a dentist."

He said, "I will change. I will put medicine as my first choice." But he then added, "I don't think I have a chance though as it's very difficult to enter medical school."

However, he was accepted to study medicine, and he got the first choice of the university he chose—Adelaide University. He studied, worked, and got his degree. After that he did his postgraduate course to be an anesthetist. Then after three years he switched to family practice. Today he is a successful medical practitioner with two private practices.

Wilfrid was eight years younger than Alex. He, too, graduated from high school with straight A's. I went with Wilfrid to meet with his school counselor who said Wilfrid should study law.

He then added, "Mr. Jaksic, what more would you wish but to have a doctor and a lawyer in the family."

Why did the counselor give this advice? Wilfrid was excellent in arguing, particularly with the evolution theory lecturers. He made it so difficult for them that they ordered him to sit in the very last row in the class. In addition, he was not allowed to say one word or he would be expelled from the class. No doubt, the student counselor was aware of Wilfrid's qualities as a strong opposer of the evolution theory and the power of his arguments.

However Wilfrid, like Alex, had different ideas. He wanted to be a doctor and study medicine. Against Alex's and our advice, he applied and was accepted to the medical school at Adelaide. Once he graduated from Adelaide University, he went on to do postgraduate courses at Adelaide University, Oxford in England, and the University of Toronto in Canada. He is now practicing hematology, the study of the physiology of blood.

When it was our sweet daughter's turn, we wondered what career would she choose?

She loved animals and always wanted to help them, especially the sick ones, so it was decided she would be a veterinary surgeon. Being also a straight-A student, she applied to study at Sydney University since Adelaide did not offer veterinary studies. She was accepted in the first intake, but after learning what was involved in the program and that she would have to go to slaughterhouses to study the effects on the animals, she felt she could not do it. So she applied to medical school as her brothers.

Against the advice of the whole family, she set her mind on medicine and was accepted at Adelaide University. During her years at university, she received a number of awards in various subjects. After graduating, she practiced in Sydney and Adelaide, and now she is practicing medicine in a private practice in Adelaide.

We thank the Lord for our children who were brilliant students and who are our pride and joy, not only because they are highly successful but because they are wonderfully caring individuals who are dedicated to helping those in need. Today they are engaged in their professions, while at the same time honoring us as parents and being a blessing to the community in which they serve.

We are also proud grandparents. Wilfrid and his wife have three wonderful children, two daughters and a son. Esther and her husband have two lovely children, a boy and a girl. Alex on the other hand is still single but has given himself financially to help the church, his parents, and others in need. Our grandchildren are our precious treasures whom we dearly love.

Chapter 27

Meeting Her Majesty Queen Elizabeth

Besides studying medicine, all three of our children studied music.

Alex studied piano for five years. Wilfrid took piano for three years and viola for five years. Esther played violin for five years and the piano for twelve years, graduating with honors in Pianoforte at Adelaide University. Esther's passion is classical music—she owns a grand piano and often plays her favorites. On the other hand, Alex plays piano at church when the need arises.

However, it was Wilfrid who made the most interesting marks during his years of playing the viola. He played in the school string orchestra and formed his own string quartet. One year while playing in the school orchestra, Queen Elizabeth II visited Australia and stopped at the school where Wilfrid was a student. The orchestra had been preparing for weeks to play in the queen's honor. Finally, the big day arrived. The members of the orchestra received thorough instruction on how to behave and how to respond if Her Majesty should speak to one of them. They were to address her as "Your Majesty," and then answer whatever she may ask.

The conductor told them it was a great honor that the queen was visiting their school and it would be an even greater honor should she speak to some members of the orchestra. We, the parents of the members of the orchestra, received special permission to be in close proximity to the orchestra, thus being in the first line as Her Majesty came out of the Rolls Royce.

As the car stopped, the man in attendance opened the door, and she got out, followed by her attendants. Then the orchestra started playing "God Save The Queen." As she moved close to the orchestra, she and the whole party stopped to listen to their performance. When they finished the conductor curtsied to the queen and exchanged greetings. Then to everybody's surprise Her Majesty took a few steps forward and stopped where Wilfrid was playing. By now all the members of the orchestra were standing.

Then the queen addressed Wilfrid by asking him, "How long have you been playing the violin?"

To which Wilfrid responded in his normal calm way without any sign of nervousness, "Actually, this is a viola that I am playing."

"Oh," the queen said, "and how long have you been playing the viola?"

"Three years," he responded.

"And are you enjoying playing?"

"Yes, very much," Wilfrid responded.

To which, Her Majesty, before moving on, said, "Keep up the good work."

"Thank you, Your Majesty," Wilfrid said.

After the queen had left, there was an assembly at the school in which all the students and the faculty were present. The principal gave his opening speech, the main topic being the visit to the school by Her Majesty the Queen.

However, before finishing his speech, he said, "It does not often happen that one of our students reprimands the Queen of England, the Queen of Australia. Wilfrid Jaksic has done just that." To this, the whole student body and every member of the faculty responded in a great uproar of prolonged applause.

For a long time after many students asked Wilfrid, "And how long have you been playing the violin?"

Chapter 28

Going "Home"

I had left Yugoslavia in 1959 to avoid conscription into the army, and after immigrating to Australia, I received nine years imprisonment in my absentia, which meant I could not go back to Yugoslavia in that time or as long as the system existed. This resulted in me not being able to return to my home country for twenty years.

It was in 1979 that my oldest brother, George, who was still a communist party member, wrote me a letter and sent a booklet that documented that the Yugoslavian government had granted amnesty to a number of people who had left Yugoslavia illegally. The amnesty did not include any war criminals or people who committed any crimes, but it granted amnesty to people who were born just before the war who had no criminal record and who were under thirty years of age when they left. I fit into that category.

It was almost too much for my limited mind to comprehend, but I could finally travel back to Yugoslavia to see my family. With this new knowledge, we began making plans to return for a visit. Then the day finally arrived when we took off from Australia and flew to Frankfurt, Germany, where Mary's sister Susi and brother-in-law Frederich, whom she has not seen for twenty-three years, met us. They came with their two children, Martin and Markus, who now reside in Australia. At our reunion tears flowed like a river. We stayed with them for some time before renting a car in Germany, packing our bags, and starting the drive to Yugoslavia.

We traveled to Austria and then to Yugoslavia. When I saw a big sign pointing to "YUGOSLAVIA," I was tempted to turn back and stay in Western Europe where freedom was the way of life. However, something urged me to continue.

As we approached the Yugoslavian border, without thinking about what effect it would have on my family, I said, "I am still free. I do not know will happen once I cross the border."

This caused my daughter much distress, and she started crying and urging me to turn back, for she was fearful that I would go to prison. It took a lot of effort to calm her down and to assure her that nothing would happen and that I would be free as I was in Austria or Australia. There was no need to be concerned.

I did not realize that, even though it was still under the communist regime, the rules in Yugoslavia had changed dramatically as far as freedom was concerned. People were able to obtain passports without any effort, even the young men who did not yet go to the army. The schools operated five days a week, and though the army was still compulsory, there were choices for those who had religious beliefs. I learned all these things as I talked with my brothers, especially with George who was still a communist party member.

As we arrived at the border, the inspections were more of a formality than military style checkpoints as it used to be. It took no longer then five to ten minutes before we crossed the border into Yugoslavia without any difficulties. That was indeed a great surprise for me, since I remembered what I had to go through twenty years earlier. We traveled through Slovenia, Croatia, and then on to Serbia. As we approached Belgrade, I felt my heart beating faster virtually wanting to jump out of my chest. I had to stop for a while and rest.

We continued our journey toward another city, Novi Sad. We had to pass through Stara Pazova where our church had a building that could seat 700 people. Despite wanting to, we did not stop as I had notified my brother Predrag of the day of our arrival, and I was determined to arrive as planned. As we passed through Beshka, which was only five kilometers from Krcedin where this "ugly baby" was born, a mix of emotions and memories flooded my mind. Wonderful, awesome, tragic, sad, poor, and cruel memories, but best of all I remember it as a place where a loving and caring mother raised me. A place where I went to school and made many friends, and a place where I was expelled from school for standing up for my beliefs.

As we arrived at the outskirts of the town and saw a big sign with the name "KRCEDIN" on it, my mind still would not accept that it was a reality. It had been now more than twenty years since I had walked from that place on foot through the fields saying goodbye to the dearest people I knew on this earth. Now I was back. In a very short time, I would be embracing my dear family members whom I had not seen or held for so long.

My mind quickly raced, and I wondered whom I would see first. Was the old house still the same as when I had left it? And the people? I had seen my mother when she was in Australia, but it had been a few years since I had last seen her. But I hadn't seen my brothers, oldest sister, uncles, cousins, neighbors, and so on.

Buried in my thoughts, I snapped back to the present as I entered the street where my house was. Then I saw number 75 with the gates wide open and many people on the street and in the frontcourt where many years ago my parents had been married. Then as we got to the little bridge, I had to turn to the right, drive over it, and for the last few meters drive into the courtyard. As I drove in, there were so many people around the car I had difficulty opening the door. We all got out, and there were loud cries of joy, "Dobro doshli, dobro doshli" meaning "welcome, welcome."

My immediate thoughts were to kiss the ground as I had seen someone important do when he went back to his native country of Poland. However, I had no chance as my family overwhelmed me. The first

The Vacant Seat

to greet me was my mother, then Predrag, George, Branka, and finally, my father. He looked old and different. He embraced me and immediately asked if it would be possible for me to forgive him. I told him all was forgiven without condition, and holding me firmly in his embrace, he cried uncontrollably.

Others arrived, many of them I did not recognize.

I felt like kissing the ground, I felt like calling from the top of my voice, "I am home, finally home. Let the whole world hear; I have returned after twenty years."

Then my brother led us inside where he and his wife, Vera, had prepared a banquet. Many tables were set out, and at least thirty people participated in this celebration for the return of a long separated brother. All my cousins, nephews, and nieces were there. It was absolute euphoria.

Regarding my father, I was particularly happy to see him. For a long time I had prayed to God that He would keep him alive so that I could meet him and get to know him. With the firm hand of my older brother, he had stopped drinking alcohol.

The days of our stay were filled with meeting people and visiting relatives and friends. We also went to the local cemetery where my uncles and some other relatives were buried. What was most surprising for me was that some of my school friends had already died and were buried in the ground.

Our children had the time of their lives with their cousins. Although it was difficult to communicate, it did not stop them from enjoying each other's company. Our Wilfrid, however, had different interests. My cousin was growing pigs, and Wilfrid was fascinated with them. Every day he went with Uncle Misha and helped him feed and clean them. Every night he had to be scrubbed clean and his clothes washed. But it was all great fun for him.

Esther was interested in improving the lot of undernourished dogs and cats that Uncle Predrag had around his house, telling him that he must look after them when we were gone. If those animals could talk, they would have begged Esther either to stay to look after them or to take them with her.

Alex had no difficulty communicating with his cousins Brane and Zoran whom he met for the first time. Fortunately, they could speak some English, and he knew some Serbian he had learned from my mother when she was with us in Australia. His cousins were of similar age as he.

It was the beginning of August, and the weather was almost perfect, warm and mild, and the fields were laden with wheat and corn almost ready for harvest. The gardens were laden with vegetables and magnificent watermelons. This time, however, there was no pact with my dear sister to take the biggest one from our neighbor, but one thing I could not resist was getting up early in the morning and going to my mother's vegetable garden and picking some fresh green leaves to eat. Oh! What a wonderful taste it was.

While I was visiting, I decided to show photos of Australia to my friends and family who were still living in Yugoslavia. I had brought only a projector and about a thousand photos of our home, garden, the flowers around our home and hills, and other scenery.

Going "Home"

So, after arriving and resting in my brother's house, I told my sister-in-law about the photos. My brother didn't have a screen, so instead we used a large white sheet pinned to the wall in the lounge room.

They invited as many relatives and neighbors as possible to view the show, and because there were so many who wanted to see, we had to hold a number of sessions so everyone could fit in the room. It was an absolute success, and everyone marveled at the beauty of Australia. I also had photos of Mary's home in Germany and of the countries we had traveled through—France, Italy, and a few others—to get to Yugoslavia.

On our last session, a relative of ours who lived at the other end of town asked me if I could show the pictures in her house so she could invite her neighbors to see the pictures. We arranged a time and went to her house, again using a large white sheet pinned to the wall. Many people came, and again we had to hold more than one session. Everyone was excited to see the pictures.

On the last night, an elderly woman came in. She had never seen television, picture shows, or anything like it. As she entered the room, I noticed she looked rather startled. As she sat, her eyes opened very wide, and she appeared as though she was in some kind of a trance. Her face was ashen white, and she never moved. I thought maybe she wasn't well and wondered if she needed a glass of water. As the show ended, she very anxiously asked my relative,

"Dorothy, whose sheet is this?"

My aunt answered, "It is mine."

The lady was even more startled and exclaimed quite loudly,

"I didn't know that you had such a sheet! How long have you had it?"

It was then that we realized this poor old lady had believed it was the sheet that was producing these "magic" pictures. Of course, we told her the truth, but it was something my children never let me live down, and every time we talk about that first trip back to my village, which is home to a "sophisticated and well-educated society", they joke about their "dad from the magic sheet village."

Chapter 29

The New Church

During our visit we had the privilege of attending the dedication of a new church building my mother had financed and my brothers had designed and built. Church members in our town had always met in private homes. While in Australia, Mother saved enough money to build the church, which included a portion of her Australian pension. The dedication was indeed a very wonderful and solemn occasion attended not only by ministers and church people but by many relatives who had never been to any church, some of them were even communist party members, including my brother George.

The church choir from Belgrade was there to lift their voices in praising the heavenly Father for this most wonderful occasion. After the dedication, Predrag and Vera invited us all over for a very wonderful vegetarian dinner. The whole occasion was unforgettable.

During our stay I had the privilege of presenting the gospel message to many of my relatives who were communist party members since their youth and had never read the Bible or attended any religious meetings. The message had a wonderful impact on some of them.

One of the most wonderful experiences I had was when George asked me to read him something from the Bible. It took me a while to think and pray about what to read that would help him find God. The obvious choice seemed to be to read about Christ, but the Lord impressed me to read from Revelation 13.

After reading it through, he asked me to explain to him what it all meant. I told him, "The first beast represents the papal power, the second beast represents the United States of America, and these two powers will unite for a while and rule the world."

My brother's reaction was very swift and resolute. "Never," he said, "you are wrong my brother. The Soviet Union is a mightier power than the USA." He went on to tell me that he had been to the USSR many times and that I have been going to the USA and that our church interpretation of this Bible chapter was not correct.

However, he asked me, despite his strong assertion of the might of the Soviet Union, when the Soviet Union would collapse and America would gain power. I told him that I could not tell him that, but I reassured him that the Bible prophecy would be fulfilled.

I read him the Revelation prophecy in 1979. Twelve years later in 1991, the USSR was no more. Thank the Lord my dear brother lived to witness the collapse of the Soviet Union and the growth of American power. He then, by the Lord's wonderful grace, read the Word of God, accepted Jesus as his personal Savior, and both he and his wife were baptized and became members of the Lord's people on earth. They are now both resting in the grave waiting for the second coming.

After a month in Yugoslavia, we went on to Romania with Mary's mother, who came to us from Austria, to visit her relatives who still lived there. Mary's grandparents accepted the Advent message in 1911, and when World War I broke out, they were among those who stood faithful to the teachings of the SDA Church. It was good to visit all Mary's relatives who, despite the communist system of government, lived reasonably comfortable lives.

From Romania, we traveled to Austria where we stayed with her parents. There we spent a few wonderful days before going back to Austria with her parents and relatives then on to Germany where we spent a short time with her sister Susi and her husband and children before returning to Australia.

Chapter 30

Working in the Pacific Region

It was in 1991 that the Lord called me to be a first-time delegate representing the Australian Union at the SDARM General Conference (GC) delegation session. I had never attended such a gathering, so I asked one of the leading ministers who had attended GC sessions previously what I would do once there. He told me to be attentive and learn the process and working of such a gathering. For me it was a wonderful, and at the same time, fearful experience.

At my very first GC session, the Lord called me to work for the young people worldwide. Despite trying to decline this awesome responsibility, the brethren elected me, and the Lord gave me strength to work with them for eight years. It was a very humbling and educational experience. While engaged in this work, the Lord gave me a wonderful opportunity to conduct international seminars, youth congresses, workshops, while generally getting acquainted with the needs and aspirations of the youth in our churches.

They were able to meet others from different parts of the world and exchange thoughts and ideas regarding the issues facing them that they have to deal with. I traveled widely among Australia, Europe, the Americas, Africa, and Asia.

Having done this, my advice to all youth workers is do not underestimate the strength, intelligence, or moral worth of the young people in our churches. They are God's precious flock, and at the same time, they are the future leaders in this vast work the Lord has called us to finish.

Then the Lord called me to work in the Pacific region for twelve years as the regional secretary. The Pacific region is a vast territory with very diverse nationalities, cultures, colors, and traditions. It was a challenge I did not anticipate.

It stretched from the middle of the Pacific Ocean with all its islands, starting with the French Polynesian islands, to the middle of Asia, including China, Vietnam, Mongolia, and the Korean peninsula to name a few. It was only by the Lord's power that I was able to work for so many years. To not only work dutifully but also to love and thoroughly enjoy it and meet the challenges along the way was nothing short of a miracle.

One of the most challenging countries in that region was China. The message of reformation had just entered the country, and the brethren decided to send me there, not to live but to visit on a regular basis two to three times a year. It was one of the greatest challenges I have experienced in my life.

On planning my first visit, I was refused a visa. I applied in Australia, and the Chinese consular office called me for an interview. The first question they asked was why I wanted to go to China. I told them that I liked China and wanted to meet Chinese people. They said there were many Chinese people in Australia and I could meet them every day if I was so interested in them.

They kept asking me for the real reason. What was my profession? What was my work? Fortunately, by then I had my own registered clothing manufacturing company, and when I filled in the visa application, I listed my position as director of the company. Despite all that, I was refused a visa.

As vice president of the GC, I often had to leave for Europe to attend conferences, so while in Yugoslavia on one of those trips, I applied for a visa at the Chinese Embassy in Belgrade. I was asked the same questions I had been asked in Australia. I gave the same answers, and again I was refused a visa. From Yugoslavia I went to Bulgaria, and while in Sofia, I applied again for a visa at the Chinese Embassy.

They asked even more questions about my intent to go to China. I told them the same thing I told the officials in Australia and Yugoslavia. But this time they were more willing to listen. Then, still not convinced of my story, they asked me to produce a letter from the Australian Embassy in Belgrade confirming my evidence I gave them. I called the Australian Embassy and explained my situation and the need of a letter from them. They were sympathetic to my situation but could not help me as I was in Bulgaria.

I would need to go back to Belgrade and talk to them personally, and then they would issue me the letter I needed. The problem was I could not go back to Yugoslavia. I decided to pray more earnestly about the situation, something I should have done from the very beginning. I started to doubt whether it was the Lord's will I should go to China since it was a communist country and was very restricted. If I went, I would be the first person from a Western country to visit the little group that was forming as part of our church. What would make it even more difficult was the fact that our church in China was not registered.

While in Bulgaria I was fortunate to have the help and support of our Bulgarian brethren, especially of one young brother by the name of Zoro Nikolov (George Nicholson) who now resides in Australia.

I met this young man at the youth convention in Hungary in 1995. He had also attended the international youth congress in Italy in 1994, but at that meeting, because of my very busy schedule, I had not been able to talk with him. At that time he was working for the Yugoslavian Union. He was indeed a wonderful help to me, so much so that without him it would have been almost impossible for me to accomplish all that needed doing. While working with the young people for eight years, the Lord helped me to form close bonds and trust with many of them, and Zoro offered his unreserved help.

The Vacant Seat

After talking to the Australian Embassy over the telephone and getting no results, I told Zoro, "Let us pray to the Lord differently than we have prayed until now. Let us ask the Lord if it is His will for me to go to China. If it is, then He will make them give me the visa. However, if it is not His will, then He will prevent them from giving me the visa."

We then earnestly prayed, and with the same application and documents, minus the letter from the Australian Embassy in Belgrade, we went to the Chinese Embassy in Sofia and submitted the application. This time I requested to talk to the consul personally. After hearing my story, the consul told me I would have to wait ten days while all my documents would be sent to Beijing. Once they were returned, they would notify me if I got the visa.

I had no choice but to wait in Bulgaria, which prevented me from going to Romania where I was to participate in the delegation and the spiritual conference of the Romanian Union.

After ten days I went to the embassy. The consul gave me all my documents, opened my passport on the page where the visa was printed, and simply said, "Your visa." I was beside myself. I thanked her very much, and in the car my young brother Zoro and I offered earnest prayers of thanks to our heavenly Father.

A few days later I was on my way to China. It was indeed a historic day not only for me but also for the church and for our Chinese brethren that at that time were few in number. I traveled to China with another young brother Jaime from Brazil, who was also a wonderful help while I worked in the South American countries. He was not only a brother in Jesus but a wonderful friend with whom to share my joys and difficulties in the Lord's work. I could not speak any of their languages, so he was my "Aaron" while I worked with the Portuguese- and Spanish-speaking young people.

When we arrived at the Shanghai airport, we saw our names "JAKSIC and CAMPOS" held high by a very attractive young Chinese woman. When we went to her, she welcomed us to the People's Republic of China and told us that during our stay in China she would be our guide.

After collecting our bags, she directed us to a waiting car with a driver wearing white gloves. As we drove to our hotel, she asked us many questions as to why we were visiting China and what our profession was. Brother Campos answered that he was a publisher. As for me, she seemed to be more interested in my work, asking me many details and reasons for coming to China.

My answers were simple, that I worked in the clothing industry and my interest was in seeing the manufacturing work in China.

"Do you plan to open an office here in Shanghai?"

"Yes. Perhaps someday," I replied.

My thoughts, of course, were that with the Lord's help we might even open a church office someday. She went on to tell us that she would look after us during our whole stay in China. My thoughts went to my brethren. I needed to meet them and be with them. When Jamie and I arrived in Shanghai, one of our brethren from South Korea arrived at the same time. We saw him at the airport, but we did not greet each other. He knew the hotel we were going to stay at, and when our guide left us with the assurance she would be back in the morning, we settled in the hotel.

Not long after there was a knock on the door. When we opened it, we were in a state of unspeakable joy. There was our brother from Korea with two Chinese brethren. When I saw the Chinese brethren, we invited them in and very warmly embraced. Soon after, they told us to go to a meeting place where more than sixty brethren had gathered to meet us and hear a message from us.

It was extremely difficult for me to have to tell them that we could not go with them. They were rather perplexed, but before they left, I told them to come the next evening and we would go with them. That night I could not sleep. I spent many hours in prayer asking the Lord to make it possible for us to go to our brethren.

The next day our guide came while we were still having our breakfast. She was very keen to take us around the city. As soon as we were ready, we got in the car with her, and we spent all day sightseeing. Just before we got out of the car after returning to the hotel, I asked her if she would be so kind to let us be by ourselves for the next four to five days since we would like to visit some shops and sightsee at our own pace. After a few questions as to why we wanted to be by ourselves, to our joy she said it would be all right. She then said that two days before our departure she would come back to take us around. We thanked the Lord for His providence. We could not have asked for more, for now we would be able to be with our brethren.

In the evening as arranged, our brethren came, and we accompanied them to meet the gathered group. Again I felt as if I was not on this planet. After greeting all the brethren, the Lord gave me words to speak to them. I cannot recall speaking with such joy and power as on that evening. The whole visit was a great wonder, a joy that is difficult to explain.

For the next eight years, I made regular trips to visit our Chinese brethren, and with each visit I walked away with a new and wonderful experience.

Chapter 31

Experiences

I will recall three different experiences I had while in China.

I grew to love our Chinese brethren with all my heart. Not only our brethren in the church, but I grew to love the Chinese people and the country as a whole. The hospitality was wonderful, and I greatly appreciated the exotic ways of doing things, the diversity of style, and the whole way of life.

Shanghai, a city of 17 million people, is very dynamic and rich in culture. Every time I went there I felt as if I was returning home. I must admit that since I am retired and no longer go there, I miss China and our brethren very much.

I was invited to preach in what is the largest Adventist Church in China. That one church has one thousand members. At the time when the invitation came, I was in the United States attending some of our church meetings. When I received the invitation to go to present our message, I consulted with some of the brethren, and they agreed that I should go. Upon arrival in Shanghai, three of my brethren and I hopped on another plane and flew to the city where the church is located. We arrived at the church just as the Sabbath School was beginning. When the pastor saw us, he received us very warmly. After taking us to the office, he wrote down our names and asked how we wanted to be introduced. I told him I prefer to be introduced simply by my name. He told me I would present the message in the afternoon.

After the morning service, we ate lunch and rested for about one hour. At about 2:30 in the afternoon I began to present the message. During my presentation, I noticed there were a number of young people, mainly young women, who were taking notes. I was presenting the 1888 message of Christ our Righteousness. By the expression on their faces, I felt they had never heard this wonderful message before.

I had been preaching for about forty minutes when my interpreter whispered to me that the pastor seemed rather agitated and was going in and out of the church. I told her to pray, and I continued my presentation. It was not even five minutes after the sister told of her concern that the pastor came in and called out "Stop. Stop. The police are here."

What happened next I had never experienced or witnessed in my life. The back wall of the church was actually a big gate. As soon as the pastor called out, the big back door opened, and the whole congregation fled. The pastor called to me at the top of his voice "You stay here," pointing to me, and then he pointed to my translator, "You stay here, too."

Out of about 300 to 350 people that had been present a few minutes ago, only five remained, the pastor, my translator, the head elder, a young man, and me. All others had fled, including three of my brethren. Soon after that the police entered the room. We stood as they entered, and we did not sit until all of them sat.

The chief of police introduced herself with a number of titles, and then she proceeded to introduce the other nine individuals with her. There were eight men and two women. She then asked me to produce my passport, and as I handed it to her, she put it in her bag. Now I had no passport.

My translator asked me, "Brother, what will happen to us?" I told her just to pray.

The chief went on to say that for such an offense (a foreigner preaching in China) I could be arrested, thrown in prison, and interrogated. But she then informed me that she planned to interrogate me first and then take me to prison. Then she asked me if I had anything to say. I told her that I was in her country and that she knew the rules. She had the power and could act accordingly. I told her that I had no power but that I had my faith in God and an inner peace in believing in Jesus Christ.

She asked me why I believed in Jesus Christ since according to her opinion Christ was not God but just an ordinary man. Then she added, if He even existed. I told her that I respected her belief but that I believed and followed Christ and that I would like to show her from my Bible as to why I had chosen to follow Christ's teaching.

Then I said, "But before I can do that I am asking for your permission to show it to you from my Bible. If I take out my Bible, which I have in my bag, and start reading to you, you could arrest me immediately and take me to prison for preaching in China. But if you give me permission to show it to you from the Bible, I will read only three words spoken by Jesus."

Now she was in a dilemma. It was a challenge. She looked at the other officers; there was tension and all kept silent. I watched them very carefully. Without anyone saying a word, I noticed their body language, and they started nodding their approval that she should let me read from the Bible. Finally she said, "Yes, you can read. I will not arrest you for that." It was a triumph for the Lord.

I took my Bible out and read from Matthew 5:44 but just three words; "Love your enemies."

As I finished reading, I could tell she was visibly moved.

Then I went on to say, "If the whole world rejected all of Christ's other teachings but followed these three words, there would be no wars, no bloodshed, no crime, no enmity, no suffering, no people like Hitler.

"If NATO forces followed these words of Jesus, they would not have bombed Belgrade, the capitol of Yugoslavia, and in the process killed and maimed thousands of innocent people. They would not have bombed your magnificent embassy in Belgrade and would not have killed two of your staff. There would be peace on earth that the whole world longs for, including the government of China." Then I stopped.

The Vacant Seat

I then looked at her and all the other police officers. There was total silence in the room. She appeared stunned. After a while she turned to my translator and spoke to her in Chinese for a long time. She then asked me more questions about my family, especially my children and what they did for work. I told her they were all three medical practitioners. She seemed surprised and then asked me if all three of them believe in Jesus? I said, "Yes, all three are Christians."

Finally, after nearly four hours of questioning, she stood up and the rest of the police followed suit, as did we. Then, instead of putting handcuffs on my hands to take me to prison, she took my passport out of her bag, handed it to me, and said, "You are free to go." I was stunned.

As she and the other officers left, she turned to me and said, "No more preaching in China, no church organizations, no ordaining elders or ministers, no religious meetings."

Later my translator told me, "Brother Jaksic, you are the best lawyer I have ever met."

I told her I was not a lawyer but that our heavenly Father, or heavenly lawyer, Jesus Christ, had fought for us and won.

On another occasion, sixty-five delegates were meeting to determine the organization of the union since the outgoing president was about to step down and other offices needed to be filled. As I was about to chair the meeting, two police officers burst in. I immediately sat down, and the police started counting the people.

Interestingly, where I was sitting there was a door leading to another room where five of us were staying. Soon after I sat down, the door opened and a brother grabbed me by the sleeve. I quickly went into that room, and my translator came with me. Then the brethren suggested I lay in bed. I said, "No, should the police come here they will easily discover me." No sooner had I said the words when there was a sharp knock on the door. I told the sister to open the door and I would stand behind it. As she opened the door, the police spoke in Chinese in rather raised voices, "What is going on here, what meeting is this, and who is the owner of this place?"

Before my translator could reply, the sister who owned the apartment came up behind the police. She told them, "I am the owner, and if you want to know what is going on come with me and I will tell you." She then led them downstairs and across the courtyard into her kitchen. She then locked the kitchen door and put the key in her pocket. Shortly thereafter, the brethren came, took me across the yard, and locked me in a small room next to the kitchen.

The situation was becoming more and more interesting by the minute. Our sister had the police locked in the kitchen and I locked in a small room next to the kitchen. I could hear the police shouting at the sister, but I could not hear her voice. After about half an hour the kitchen door opened, and the police left.

Soon after the brethren came and told me, "Brother, the police are coming back soon with at last ten other officers to arrest us all. But before they arrive, you have to finish organizing the union, and then we will take you out of here."

What came to my mind were the words of that lovely hymn "Courage Brother." I prayed to the Lord to give me wisdom on how to organize this rather large union in such a short time (about an hour), if that long. As I approached the front, I asked for prayer, and after reading a few Bible texts, I proceeded with the organization of the union. It was the fastest union organization meeting I have ever chaired.

I simply posed a question to all the delegates. "How many agree that all the officers of the last two years be re-elected for the next two years?"

All hands went up. Then I asked how many opposed the motion. One hand went up. "Carried." Then I called the president and all the officers forward and wished them the Lord's blessings and courage. After an earnest prayer, I told the Chinese brethren I had to leave.

It was a heartbreaking experience. I grew to love these dear people after working with them for more than eight years. The fellowship was wonderful—the hospitality, the trust, the love. Watching the growth of the membership and dealing in their joys and sorrows left a deep impression upon me. As I was walking out of that meeting place, I could not restrain my tears.

Chinese people are well organized. As they prepared for me to leave the premises, no one panicked and there was no confusion—all seemed to run very smoothly. They put a big old farmers coat on me. Then they put what appeared to be the largest Chinese straw hat on my head, a type that they use when planting rice. I sat in the little two-wheel carriage. They put my bags next to me and covered them with cabbage and other vegetable leaves. They also put a cloth over my mouth so that only my eyes were visible. I put my hands inside the coat, and I was ready.

The big gate opened, and the two young men began to move their "cargo." One peddled the bicycle, and the other pushed the wagon. It was daylight, which was unique because I had always arrived to this place at night and left at night.

We traveled for about an hour before stopping. I tried to get up, but the young men stopped me by putting their hands on my shoulders. Then they started lifting me up under my arms. Even though I could not communicate with them in Chinese, I got the message. I was supposed to be an old Chinese man who had difficulty walking. They started lifting me out of that wagon, and I limped as they led me to the footpath. Then with their help, I sat on the pavement by the roadside. Soon after that the translator came and told me that we were still not out of danger.

We needed to get a taxi and travel eighty kilometers to a large city where there were many European business people. I asked what had happened to the rest of the brethren. She told me that when she left the police had not yet arrived. As it happened in less than fifteen minutes a taxi came, and we were able

The Vacant Seat

to hire him. In China most of the taxis have tinted windows and the drivers have an enclosure around them. I got in the back seat and one of the young men and the translator sat in the front. The other young man went away with the cart.

The journey was good. There was very little conversation between our sister and the driver who wore white gloves while driving. Most of the taxi drivers wear white gloves in China. At the end of our trip after paying the driver, we got out and the sister told me "Brother, we are okay here. As you can see there are many Europeans."

Before long I was at the hotel where I had booked a room. It felt good, but I was concerned for my brethren and for the sister who owned the apartment.

As I said goodbye to the sister whom I shall call Sister Ella, my translator, we arranged that as soon as she got any news about our brethren she would call me. I hoped that she would call me sometime in the evening, but there was no call. I waited until late into the night; sleep would not come. I spent virtually all night praying and hoping that my brethren were all safe, especially the dear sister who owned the apartment where they held the meetings.

Finally, I received word the following evening that all the brethren managed to leave before twelve police officers arrived. The sister who owned the apartment, along with her husband and two or three other sisters, moved all the boards and bricks on which we sat and brought out a large table with a few chairs in their place. They made themselves cups of herbal tea and sat down. Not long after that the police arrived. They rushed in with such force that she felt as if the house was shaking.

"Where are the people?" one of the police shouted.

"They are gone to their homes," the sister replied.

"What kind of meeting was held here?"

"Meeting?" The sister asked. "They were my friends and relatives."

The rest of the police were angry with the first two officers for leaving the place.

"One should have stayed and one should have come to notify of the meeting."

However, they did not realize a Higher Power had directed the whole situation.

By the time Sister Ella came with the report, the sister who owned the apartment was still in police custody—she was the only one they took. Sister Ella told me there was going to be an all night meeting to pray for our sister in custody. When we arrived at the place, most of the brethren had already assembled. The meeting stared about 10:00 p.m. and went until 4:30 in the morning. There was standing room only; in fact, I stood on a bed to present a message and answer any questions. Before dawn, we left.

Experiences

There was one more experience during my time in China that was a direct manifestation of the mighty hand of the Lord. One evening after some meetings, we boarded a bus for the return trip to Shanghai. But before we entered the city a police officer stopped the buses we were traveling in. As soon as the brethren saw the police officer, they told me, "Brother, lie down."

I had only two seats I could use, but I curled up into the fetal position, and they covered me with a blanket and an overcoat, which was actually nice since it was winter and there was no heating in the bus. It was a mini-bus operated by a relative of one of our brethren. There were only seven of us including the driver.

The bus stopped, and as the police officer got on, he ordered the driver to switch on all the lights, and then he ordered all the passengers to go to the front of the bus near the driver. The driver did as he requested, after which the officer proceeded from the front to the back of the bus, inspecting all the seats and turning over all the bags. With his job done, he left the bus. However, he never lifted the blanket to see what was under it. Thank the Lord for His angel who I am sure stood in front of him blocking access to my seat.

At the time of this writing, I have not been to China in more than four year. I miss my dear brethren and sisters there. I miss their hospitality, their unflinching faith, their courage, and their missionary zeal. I also miss the magnificent city of Shanghai, its shops, and their staff who almost overwhelmed me in helping me buy whatever I needed. I also miss the hotel and the staff who got to know me during my eight years of visits.

I hope to someday return to visit the brethren there again.

Chapter 32

Work in Other Pacific Region Countries

During the twelve years in the Pacific region, I endured many challenges and many wonderful and joyful experiences. The countries I worked most actively in were American Samoa, Australia, China, Fiji, French Polynesia, Japan, Mongolia, New Caledonia, New Zealand, Papua New Guinea, South Korea, Vanuatu, Vietnam, and Western Samoa.

Over the years I learned much and experienced much joy. Most of all I gained a wonderful insight into how the Lord works on the minds of people of diverse cultures, races, nationalities, and customs. Yet despite all the diversity, there can exist a complete harmony, a complete unity in Christ.

Wherever the work took me I had good experiences and thoroughly enjoyed the challenges I encountered. During my years of service, I was blessed that wherever the Lord sent me I enjoyed the love and friendship in the countries I worked in. Although I had to meet many challenges and some difficulties, the good times overrode all the hard times. I do miss my brethren and the many friends I made in that country.

When I would travel for the first time to Mongolia or Vietnam or South Korea or Japan, to name just a few, I always wondered how the people would accept the message I would be presenting to them.

For instance, after a small group was established in Mongolia, I was called to visit the believers and present more studies to them and to conduct seminars for the public. Prior to my departure from Australia, I notified Sister Bayamba who was our leader there and told her the time of my arrival. This was in February 2001, so it was summer in Australia. We had been experiencing very hot weather, and on the day I was to leave, the temperature was over 42 degrees Celsius. It was very hot indeed.

I flew from Adelaide to Sydney, then on to Beijing, China. In Beijing, I boarded a plane for Ulaanbaatar, the capital of Mongolia. After clearing customs, I was met by Sister Bayamba. Although I had never seen her before, we had corresponded, and it was a very wonderful meeting. But I felt as if I was on another planet.

They had shawls around their necks and heads, and they were wearing leather gloves. I too was dressed warm, but as we got out of the airport building, I realized I was not dressed warm enough for this climate. When I opened the door to exit the building and inhaled the extremely cold air, I lost my breath. I quickly shut the door and Sister Bayamba told me that the outside temperature was 35 degrees Celsius below zero, which was extremely cold compared to the extreme heat of Australia.

The sister took me to a shop where I bought myself warm clothes. A leather coat, shoes with real wool inside, leather gloves, shawls and a Russian cap to cover not only the top of my head but my ears and neck. When I got dressed, I must have been at least twenty kilograms heavier. I walked like the astronauts on the moon. No one could recognize me; my whole face was covered, and only my eyes were free so I could see where I was going. All the people were dressed like that. When walking on the street if you bumped into someone, you just simply rolled, even if you fell. You did not feel anything because of all the padding you had on your whole body.

Getting into a car created another problem. Since you were so bulky, you had to remove some of the clothing. However, if you were to do this outside the car, it meant freezing almost to the point of numbness. Finally, we figured out how to enter the car fully dressed and then remove the layers of clothes inside the car. For the four of us to get ready to go anywhere it took about forty minutes. Sister Bayamba spoke very little English, so she had hired a woman who spoke fluently. When we arrived at the sister's house, it was warm inside with central heating supplied by the great power stations.

On some of my trips, I witnessed heart-wrenching poverty. One time I left Australia to visit a country in the Pacific. I landed late at night in an airport that was substandard in all aspects. It was extremely hot and humid.

We had a few believers there, but we had very little communication with them as telephone contact was not always possible. Prior to leaving Australia, I was able to contact a brother on the island and tell him the flight number and the time of my arrival. He told me he would be waiting for me. When I arrived, he was not there. At first, I thought he was running late, so I waited. However, after waiting for more than an hour, he did not arrive.

Then finally a man approached me and asked me if I was Seventh-day Adventist Vegetarian. I said that I was. He told me that the man who was going to meet me sent him because he had no transportation. He told me he would take me to the place I was to go. I asked the man his name, and he told me, but I could not understand him. I offered a silent prayer and decided to go with him, putting myself in the Lord's hands.

He had a small pickup truck, and after putting my bags in the back, I sat in the cabin next to him, and we started on our trip. I refrained from asking him too many questions for fear that he would perceive that I did not fully trust him. It was dark, and the road was a bush track and very bumpy. He went

The Vacant Seat

slowly, and we traveled in silence. I tried to make some light conversation, but he did not respond. I glanced at my watch and noticed we had traveled more than an hour through a virtual jungle. I asked him how much longer we had to go, and he just said we would get there in time.

Finally, we arrived at our destination, and to my great relief, the brother who should have met me at the airport was there waiting for me with his wife. They received me warmly in front of their house, which consisted of a round concrete platform and about six posts and a thatched roof. There were no electrical lamps, only kerosene lamps, hanging on the posts giving light to the area. I saw a few children sleeping on mats made of dry leaves.

They asked if I was hungry, but I told them I was tired and would prefer to go to sleep. They took me to my house that was similar to theirs, except it had new posts and a new roof made of leaves and branches. There was no cement floor, but they had placed a foam mattress on the grass. I took out my mosquito protection net and hung it over my bed. I hung my clothes on the post that supported the roof, and after offering a prayer, I went to sleep.

I may have slept an hour or so when loud thunder and heavy rain woke me. Within minutes, my mattress was submerged in water, and before I could get up, my whole body was almost under water. My house was in a little valley, which quickly became a pond.

I got up and moved to higher ground as fast as possible. Since it was about 3:00 a.m., I just waited until the morning. Fortunately, it is very hot in the tropics, so I figured that things should dry out quickly. Mosquitoes now felt like fiery darts. I stayed under the net even if I had to stand in the water. When the brother saw my situation, he was apologetic. Together with some young people, they built me another house, this time with a raised platform for my bed about a meter off the ground. They also built me a chair and a table for my books. Now I had a more comfortable home than they did.

I stayed with them for about ten days and studied with many people who came to listen to the Word of God.

It was always a challenge and joy to visit New Caledonia. The official language was French, and if you did not speak it or their native language, you were in real trouble as most of them did not speak English. On a number of occasions, I went with Brother Balbach Senior. He spoke French, and they told me his French was better than theirs was. He was without doubt a scholar in the true sense of the word.

It was a blessed time there together as we conducted seminars, workshops, answered questions, went for walks, and discussed the culinary excellence of our brethren. However, there were times when I had to go without Brother Balbach, which meant I had no translator other than one sister who spoke fluent English and would sometimes translate for me. One particular time when I was visiting them, they said there was nobody to translate as Brother Balbach could not go and the sister who could speak English was on a journey. The brother who told me this spoke very little English and not enough to translate.

He told me we could hire a translator from a company that had professional translators, but we would have to pay on hourly rate. We agreed to get someone since without being able to communicate my visit was in vain.

As it happened, a woman arrived who spoke excellent English and I thought that our problem was resolved. However, when I asked how much she would charge us per hour for seven days of full meetings, her answer caused my head to spin. It would cost more to have her translate than my return trip to Australia, including cost for accommodations and food.

"No, no," I told the brother with little English, "send her away. We cannot afford to pay her."

"But who will translate?" he asked.

Then came faith or presumption. Perhaps I committed a sin of presumption, but I told the brother if no one came to translate that the Lord would give me the gift of the French language and I would speak to them in French. He was astonished, and I could see on his face a real expression of concern. He must have questioned and likely doubted my sanity and if he could trust me.

I then told him to call all the people together so that we could start the meeting. He got even more worried.

When I told him to come to the front with me, he said, "No, no, I cannot translate, no Brother Jaksic, I cannot translate."

"Come with me and we will start the meeting."

He then came and announced the hymn to be sung, and we all knelt in prayer. After the prayer we sat down. He then turned and looked at me, but this time anxiety was written all over his face, and I became concerned that he may suffer heart failure. I told him to ask the congregation to sing another hymn. By now, I too was waiting for the Lord to show His power on our behalf.

During the singing of the second hymn, a miracle happened. A young couple who were visitors from the local SDA Church walked in.

The brother whispered to me, "They speak English".

The Lord was working on behalf of His people. I then addressed the visitors. I welcomed them in English and told them I believed the Lord had sent them. They relayed that they, too, believed the same. I told them the Lord had sent them here for two reasons: one to hear the message of reformation and the second to be like Aaron for me since I did not speak French and no one spoke English good enough to translate.

I asked if they would show us kindness and translate for me during my stay in New Caledonia, a whole week of meetings. Without any hesitation, they responded they would be glad to help us. They

The Vacant Seat

both could not be there for every meeting, but they made sure that one of them was always there. The Lord still works miracles for His people. We all had a very blessed time.

My travels also took me to South Korea. "Brother, you should become a citizen of South Korea" was what my South Korean brethren would often tell me. I visited them so often that Korea became a home away from home. Working for and with the brethren in Korea was indeed a wonderful experience. If you wish to experience hospitality and warm friendships, go to South Korea.

In Japan I learned the value of true dedication to the cause of Christ that the Japanese people believed in and stood for. They were not many in number, but with their efforts and hard work, they accomplished more than one could imagine. They built a magnificent church that when one sees it, and knowing the few there, then one cannot help but be astonished. Here I had the privilege to work with these dear hard-working people and their minister and his dear wife, with whom I am not only a brother in faith but also a dear and valued friend.

In French Polynesia if you want to do well financially, you grow watermelons and sell them to the numerous hotels and thousands of tourists that visit the islands every year. Here again it was a privilege to work in the warm, pleasant climate, making it an ideal place to work and make friends for the kingdom.

One time in Vanuatu I was attending a field conference and delegation session. After one of the meetings in which I was presenting the topic of Christ our Righteousness, a man came to me and told me that he was a member of the Adventist Church on the Solomon Islands. He told me he had never heard such a message before and that he would like me to go to the Solomon Islands and present the same message. He told me I should let him know of the time of my arrival before I could even tell him that my coming to the Solomon Islands would have to be approved by the Australian Union committee, or rather I would have to be sent there. I told him that on my return to Australia, I would talk to the brethren, and I would let him know. He went on to say that he would hire a large hall and invite as many people as possible, "This message must be heard by the people there."

After talking to the brethren in Australia, they agreed to send me to the Solomon Islands. Before going, I called the brethren in Vanuatu and asked them if someone could come with me since they have similar cultures and language. They agreed to send someone with me.

When I booked my trip, I notified the man in Vanuatu, sending him the details of my arrival date, the flight number, and the time of arrival. When we arrived at Honiara airport, after going through the normal procedures of customs and passport control, we looked for the man whom we expected to be there waiting for us. However, as the time went on and all the passengers were gone, we were still waiting for our friend to meet us. Taxi drivers kept asking us where we were going and if they could take us. We kept telling them that we were waiting for a friend to take us to a motel.

Finally, after waiting more than hour and a half, we decided to talk to the taxi driver who took the most interest in us—he must have asked us more than ten times if he could take us to a hotel or a motel. We told him to take us to a good motel since we had never been here before and were not familiar with what kind of accommodations there were. As we sat in his car, he asked us if we were missionaries. We told him that we were. He said, "I know a good motel. You will be happy there."

He took us to a motel owned by a member of the Adventist Church. Fortunately, they had room for us, but it was without air conditioning. I asked them if they could give us a room with air conditioning, and they promised a room would be available in the morning. The Solomon Islands have a very, very hot climate—it feels as if you are constantly in a sauna. Thank the Lord we had the air-conditioned room the next day as promised.

Soon after we settled into our rooms, we realized all the staff were members of the SDA Church. That gave me a wonderful opportunity to share the message of reform with these people. I also realized I had very little literature to give to them, so I got out my laptop and started writing. I wrote five different papers and printed some I had already done.

After making fifty copies of each, we proceeded to talk to the staff members and the guests, mainly young students. After introducing ourselves, we offered them the papers. To our pleasant surprise, the literature was well received. In addition, some came to us asking for more information. Finally, the owner of the motel approached me and asked me to give the literature to him, which I gladly did. By Thursday evening we had distributed about 500 pieces on ten different topics.

Late on Friday afternoon, to our surprise, the man we had been waiting for at the airport arrived. He told us the reason he had not been there was that he thought we were arriving on a later flight. He had been there to meet us at that time, but we were not there. He asked the taxi drivers if they had transported us, and the one who took us to the motel told him where we were staying.

The Vacant Seat

It was all providential since he had booked rooms for us at another motel not owned by an Adventist. He then told us he would come back in the morning, which was Sabbath, and take us to one of the churches. He told us the SDA Church was one of five largest churches on the Solomon Islands.

After talking with him for an hour, he left. He had not managed to organize any meetings, but he told me that he would ask the pastor of the church if he would allow me to speak in the afternoon. I was happy with this and prayed that the Lord would give me the opportunity to witness to the people and present the message of reformation to them.

Early on Sabbath morning he arrived and took us in his car to the church, which was in a very nice area with beautiful trees that was near the sea. Soon after arriving at the church, he introduced us to the pastor and to the elder. After talking to the pastor, the man told me they would give me time to speak in the afternoon. I was happy with that and prayed that the Lord would give me wisdom to present the message that would have an impact upon the people.

After Sabbath School, I saw the pastor, the elder, and our friend Ben who brought us having a serious conversation. I thought that perhaps the pastor had changed his mind regarding the afternoon talk that I was planning to present. After they finished their conversation, Ben came to me and told me they were expecting to have a guest speaker that day but for some reason the visiting pastor could not come. They had decided to ask me to speak at the divine service in addition to the afternoon. I believe the Lord arranged things for me to be able to speak. I prayed earnestly for wisdom from above and for the guidance of the Holy Spirit. The theme was "The 1888 Message: The Work and the Mission of the Angel of Revelation 18."

After the meetings, we distributed literature, which was received well. It was a wonderful day, and we were invited to come again. This meeting at the church proved to be a wonderful blessing as we continued our work in the Solomon Islands.

My next trip was three months later. This time I traveled with Andrew, another brother from Vanuatu who was a young Bible worker. A talented young man, he was energetic and full of love for the cause of God. Seeing that we needed literature, I wrote nineteen pamphlets. Thank the Lord that the literature proved to be a powerful witness for the cause of God.

Although the population of the Solomon Islands is mainly Christian, there are a lot of pagan beliefs and practices that involved voodoo, underworld spirits, calling on the dead, and many other rather frightful practices. I decided to write about the Bible truth on the state of the dead. Brother Andrew and I went through the streets of Honiara, the capital city, distributing literature to all passersby. The Lord blessed our work there.

On our third trip, we met with a brother who was on fire for the cause of God. We presented to him the message, and he decided to join the church. He was baptized and became the first member of the SDARM in the Solomon Islands.

His name is Fernandez Cruz, and he remains an untiring worker, now a Bible worker. He introduced us to many people and scheduled a series of meetings for two weeks, which resulted in six baptisms.

We decided to register our church in the Solomon Islands and were able to organize a group with the election of a leader, secretary, and treasurer. When we went to the office to apply for the registration, there was a large man with a very stern face behind the counter. Brother Fernandez whispered that the man was an Adventist. He asked us our reason for coming, and I told him that we needed an application to register a church.

"What church do you want to register?"

I told him, and he looked at me in a way that indicated that he was not delighted with my request. Nevertheless, he gave me the forms and told me to answer every question. I asked him if we needed to submit our church constitution and bylaws, but he said no.

When we went back the next day with the filled in forms, there was a young man behind the desk, also an Adventist. We handed him the papers and after reading them, he asked us, "Where is your constitution and bylaws?"

We told him the man who gave us the forms the day before said we did not need to bring them. He was rather surprised and told us that he could not proceed with the registration until we had turned in the necessary documents. It took us all afternoon to prepare the documents. When we went the third day, there was a woman with a pleasant smile who asked us if she could help us. She too was an Adventist.

I handed her all the documents, and after she thoroughly read them, she looked at me, and to my great surprise, she told me that she knew me. I asked how, as I did not recall meeting her, and she told me that she had heard me preach in her church on my first visit to the island. She also remembered the message I gave.

Then I realized it had been God's providence that I should preach in that church. I asked her when our registration could be finalized, and she said it would take three days. On the third day we went back to the office and she was there to welcome us and give us our registration documents.

Our God is a great God. He works in ways that we never expect or even plan.

Since that time, I have visited the Solomon Islands a number of times, and every time we add more souls to the church. At the time of writing this, there are now four Bible workers in the area. The people on the island are dedicated to the cause of God and reaching more people for the kingdom. It is always a joy to go and be with these enthusiastic people.

Epilogue

I could write so much more about the many experiences I have had the privilege of being a part of in this grand design of God to proclaim the love of God around the world.

This is the cup of life that God, the Creator of universe and Christ, who paid the supreme price on the cross to restore humanity to the image of God in which we were created, has given me.

During my work for the church, the Lord called me to a number of responsibilities that gave me rich experience in working with different nationalities, races, and cultures. It was wonderful to observe that, despite the diversities, all could be united in Christ. For eight years it was my privilege to work with the young people worldwide, and for twelve years I served as secretary of the Pacific region. In addition, the Lord called me to be president of the Australian Union for one term of two years.

I am now officially retired, but it is a joy to work as a volunteer while proclaiming the message God has given the church.

My life has been one of turmoil and triumph. But I thank God for the words of advice of the kind pastor who told my dear, loving mother, when in the greatest crisis and some of the darkest hours of her life, to entrust her life and the life of her unborn baby into God's hands—"If it is God's will, both you and the child will live, but if it is not His will, then either or both of you shall die."

I thank God for the life of my precious family and for the many dear and wonderful friends I have had the privilege to meet and make.

I thank Him every day.

We invite you to view the complete
selection of titles we publish at:

www.TEACHServices.com

Scan with your mobile
device to go directly
to our website.

Please write or email us your praises, reactions, or
thoughts about this or any other book we publish at:

TEACH Services, Inc.
P U B L I S H I N G
www.TEACHServices.com

P.O. Box 954
Ringgold, GA 30736

info@TEACHServices.com

TEACH Services, Inc., titles may be purchased in bulk for
educational, business, fund-raising, or sales promotional use.
For information, please e-mail:

BulkSales@TEACHServices.com

Finally, if you are interested in seeing
your own book in print, please contact us at

publishing@TEACHServices.com

We would be happy to review your manuscript for free.

www.ingramcontent.com/pod-product-compliance
Lightning Source LLC
Chambersburg PA
CBHW081923170426
43200CB00014B/2816